Ex Libris

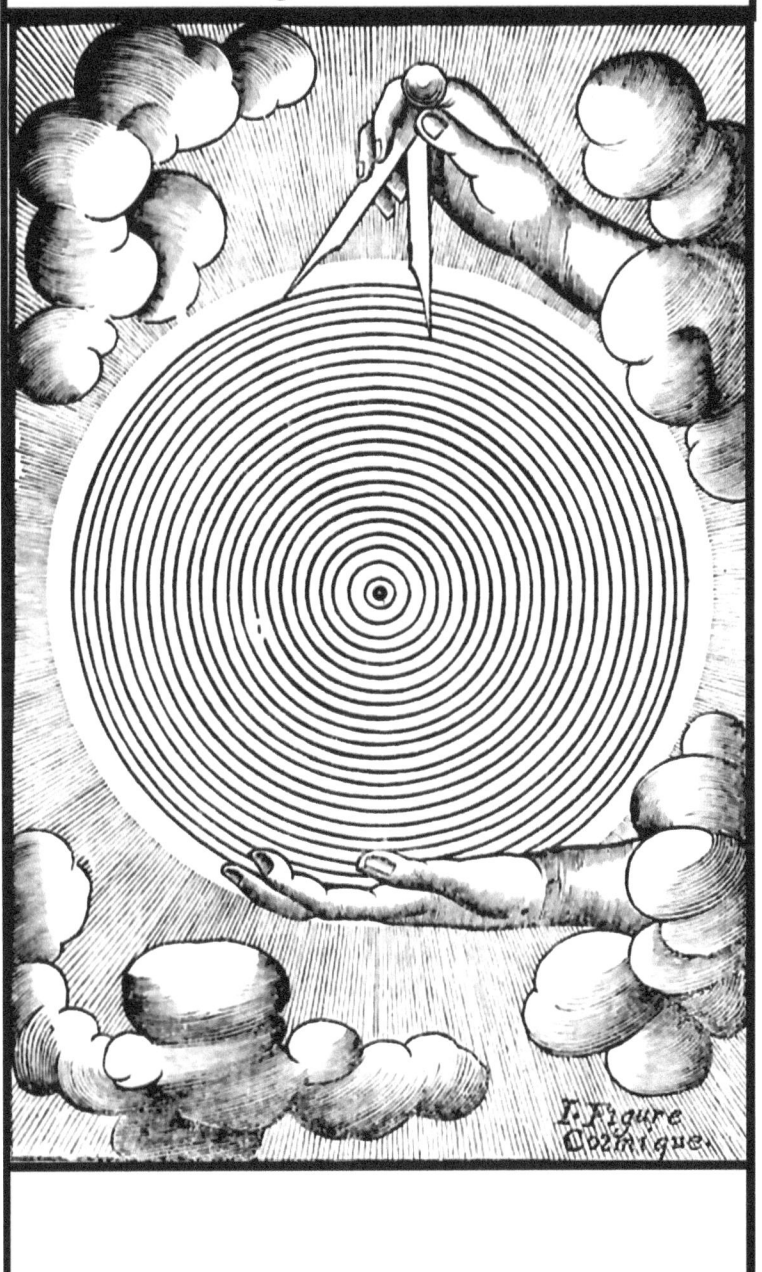

Kindest regards of
Manly P. Hall

Manly P. Hall illustrated by Jessica Naomi

Manly P. Hall A Seeker of More Intelligent Life – Book Third

Compiled with graphics and edits by Darrell Jordan, Copyright © First Edition 2023. All rights reserved.

No part of this book may be reproduced in whole or in part without the written permission from the publisher, nor stored in any retrieval system or transmitted by any means, electronic, mechanical, photocopying, recording, or other, without the written consent of the publisher.

For bulk purchases, please contact the publisher.

Enquiry@Athenaia.Co

Library of Congress Cataloging-in Publication Data

Names: Hall, Manly P. | Jordan, Darrell

Title: Manly P. Hall A Seeker of More Intelligent Life – Book Third

Description: First U.S. edition. | Coeur D'Alene, Idaho: Athenaia [2023]

Identifiers: LCCN (pending) | ISBN 979-8-88556-045-0 (First Edition hardcover)

Subjects: OCC040000: BODY, MIND & SPIRIT / Hermetism & Rosicrucianism, | PHI013000: PHILOSOPHY / Metaphysics, | SOC038000: SOCIAL SCIENCE / Freemasonry & Secret Societies

LC record available at https://lccn. loc.go

On the internet: Parallel47North.com/collections/esoteric-books

Managing Editor: Darrell Jordan

Original Author and Essay: Manly P. Hall

Executive Producer: Yuka Jordan

Book Cover Art and Illustrations: Jessica Naomi

Image Credits: Manly P. Hall's personal collection

Printed and bound in the United States

Publisher: Athenaia, LLC

2370 N Merritt Crk Lp, Ste 1

Coeur D'Alene, ID 83814

The United States

Manly P. Hall

A Seeker of More Intelligent Life

Book Third

Darrell Jordan, MPS

CONTENTS

INTRODUCTION	9
MAY 1936	11
LAO-TZE THE OBSCURE SAGE	11
THE DOCTRINE OF TAOISM	15
THE DISCIPLINES OF TAOISM	22
QUOTATIONS	23
JUNE 15, 1936	25
CONFUCIUS	25
THE DOCTRINES OF CONFUCIUS	31
CONFUCIAN DISCIPLINES	34
QUOTATIONS	36
JULY 15, 1936	37
BUDDHA	37
THE TEACHINGS OF BUDDHA	45
QUOTATIONS FROM THE DHAMMAPADA	51
AUGUST 15, 1936	52
ZOROASTER	52
THE ZOROASTRIAN DOCTRINE	59
QUOTATIONS	62
SEATTLE, WASH., SEPTEMBER 15, 1936	64
PLATO, THE DIVINE MAN	64
THE PHILOSOPHY OF PLATO	67
THE PLATONIC DISCIPLINES	72
QUOTATIONS	75
PORTLAND, OREGON. OCT. 15 1936	76
MOHAMMED, PROPHET OF ISLAM	76
THE DOCTRINES OF MOHAMMED	83
LOS ANGELES, CALIF. NOV. 1936	89
QUETZALCOATL	89

THE LIFE OF QUETZALCOATL	93
FRAGMENTS OF ANCIENT MEXICAN METAPHYSICS	100
EXTRACTS FROM AN AZTEC PRAYER	101
LOS ANGELES, CALIF. DEC. 1936	102
JESUS	102
THE TEACHINGS OF THE MASTER	110
LOS ANGELES, CALIF., JAN. 1937	116
PADMA SAMBHAVA	116
FUNDAMENTAL TENETS OF LAMAISM	122
EXTRACTS FROM TIBETAN PHILOSOPHY.	128
FEB. 15, 1937	129
AKHNATON, ADORER OF THE ATON.	129
THE RELIGIOUS TEACHING OF AKHNATON	136
QUOTATIONS FROM THE HYMNS OF AKHNATON	140
LOS ANGELES, MAR. 15, 1937	142
ORPHEUS	142
THE TEACHINGS OF ORPHEUS	149
A FEW SELECTED LINES FROM	154
THE ORPHIC RHAPSODIES	154
LOS ANGELES, APRIL, 1937	156
HERMES TRISMEGISTUS	156
QUOTATIONS	168
AUTHOR AND MANAGING EDITOR	171
MANLY P. HALL BOOK SERIES	173

INTRODUCTION

EDITOR'S NOTE

Manley Hall was born on 18 March 1901, in Peterborough, Canada, to William S. and Louise Palmer Hall. The Hall family moved to Sioux Falls, South Dakota, United States, in 1904. Manly Hall later settled in Los Angeles in 1919.

As a young man, he became interested in all forms of occult subjects. He subsequently joined a number of societies, among them the Theosophical Society, the Freemasons, the Societas Rosecruciana in Civitatibus Foederatis, and the American Federation of Astrologers.

In 1922, Hall wrote his first book: Initiates of the Flame and was collecting all form of esoteric/exoteric/mystical subject matter, in his own words: "late in the fall of 1922, the plan for a comprehensive work on the symbolism of western mystical societies began to take shape in my mind. It soon became apparent that research facilities for such a project were not available in Southern California... The only answer was to contact antiquarian book dealers and elicit their cooperation in the search for the items desired." In 1934, Hall founded the Philosophical Research Society, a research institute modeled on the ancient school of Pythagoras.

He was ordained a minister in 1923 to an occult/mystic congregation at the Church of the People in California. In that same year specifically in May 1923, Manly Hall began the membership/student based, not for sale magazine, all written, edited and published by Hall titled the "The All Seeing-Eye."

We now follow Manly P. Hall from the "All Seeing Eye" book series at the age of 24, to his private lessons for his students in this latest book series, at the age of 32. In this series, Mr. Hall moves from imparting wisdom through stories to a confident, fact-based approach of his findings and understanding of his research. His elucidation exudes confidence and is well written, with it being exceedingly broad in scope. In this series we provide 4 years of lessons condensed into four books. We are positive you will find the information herein to be quite useful in filling in some hidden areas of understanding in religion and history.

Editing was minimal in terms of punctuation and spelling. In some cases, there are made-up words (or words that are no longer in use) in which case they were left spelled as is.

I'm sure that you will find, as did I, that Manly Hall was highly intelligent and possibly bordering on genius.

Suffice it to say, we are positive you will enjoy the many journeys Manly Hall takes you on.

Darrell Jordan, MPS

MAY 1936

Dear Friend,

LAO-TZE THE OBSCURE SAGE

On a certain night in the year B.C. 604 a great falling star flashed through the heavens above what is now the Ho-nan Province of China... At that very hour a peasant Woman, weary with working in the fields of a feudal lord, gave birth to a son under a plum tree. The mother, a widow of poor circumstances, named her newborn son Plumtree and later observing the extreme length of the lobes of his ears, added the further word Ear to his name. Little Plumtree Ear was in many other respects different from other children. He was conceived, according to the tradition, without a mortal father by the influence of a great comet which was hovering over what is now Kwei-te at the hour of his conception. He—was born with a full head of long white hair and his bushy eyebrows were of the same color. Like all very small babies, he had a very old and wise look about him. The ever-wagging tongue of tradition solemnly affirmed that he was born on his own seventieth birthday.

In China all history is rapidly embellished with fantastic flights into the supernatural, but it is safe to say conservatively that little Plumtree Ear was indeed of humble parentage and obscure origin, otherwise his ancestry could not have evaded the searching eyes of Chinese historians. His youth is equally obscure, but judging from the poverty of the class into which he was born, we may assume that his struggle for education was long and difficult. The auguries of his birth predestined him to high estate in the world of learning, and to this destiny he rose triumphant above all the limitations of ancestry and opportunity.

He lived alone; he studied alone, and he meditated alone. Being deprived of the educational resources of his own country, he searched deeply within himself for the priceless secret of the ages. His very obscurity became the dominant precept of his life. So little is known of him as a personality that modern sceptics even attempt to prove that his very being is only a figment of Chinese imagination.

As years advanced upon the white-haired man honor and dignity came with them and he was appointed librarian of the Chou (the Third Dynasty extending from 1050 to 256 B. C.) This important appointment was the turning point in the philosopher's life. He emerged from the struggle for knowledge to find himself in the midst of the accumulated knowledge of the world. The third Ministry of the Chou was divided into two bodies of learned men. The first group was termed the Bureau of Annalists, and the second the Bureau of Astrologers. The duties of the Annalists were twofold. First, to record all the words and deeds of the emperor and place in an imperishable form all the laws and edicts of the state. Their second duty was to receive, arrange and record all forms of knowledge from the provinces of the empire and every other country of the civilized world. The Bureau of Astrologers devoted their lives also to two tasks. The first was to calculate all of the planetary and sidereal motions, predict eclipses and comets, and sustain and correct the calendar. Their second task was to correlate their findings with the records arranged and preserved by the Annalists, in this way checking constantly the relationship between celestial phenomena and the social and political states of man.

It is easy to understand that the frail-bodied, large-headed philosopher found in the archives of the Third Ministry the elements of his great metaphysical system. The white-haired thinker, in his simple somber robes, moved almost like a ghost through the great corridors of the library. He was always silent, always abstracted, always like some being from another world. Nothing whatever is known of his private life. He apparently married, for the names of his sons and grandsons are recorded by the Chinese historians and his descendants, like those of Confucius, shared to some measure the illustriousness of his name.

It was on the broad steps of the library of the Chou that Lao-Tze met Confucius. The Taoist philosopher was at that time near his eightieth year, Confucius was many years his junior. The meeting of the mystic and the moralist, though not historically certain, is well within the sphere of probabilities. Confucius sought the fountain-head of Chinese metaphysics. He found it in the stoop-shouldered, dark-robed man to whom all material life was illusion, all form and ceremony vanity, all honor ephemeral, and nothing real but the nameless, unknown Cause of all. Confucius retired from the interview incapable of grasping the abstractions of the Taoist sage. Confucius so loved mankind that he could perceive no greater virtue than the creation of a condition in which all men might prosper under good laws and wise rulership. Yet it would be wrong to deny that Confucius was influenced by the mystical attachment of the Taoist viewpoint. Dimly, Confucius sensed the sublimity of the Inner Way. It influenced his later writings, but he never ceased to be a humanist.

The name by which the Taoist master is now known throughout China and the civilized world is Lao-Tze, but it is doubtful if he carried this name while alive. The word Lao-Tze, meaning the Ancient Child, is of course derived from his appearance in infancy, but during his lifetime he probably went under his surname Li, meaning Plum, the plum tree being in China the symbol of immortality. The word Lao-Tze has gradually been enlarged by popular usage to include in its meaning Venerable Philosopher or Ancient Wise One.

It would be erroneous to accept Li or Lao-Tze as the founder of Taoism. The doctrine was actually a more or less formulated belief severed a hundred years before his birth. The first Taoists were almost certainly the Annalists and Astrologers of the great Chinese libraries. These men, because of their peculiar position as compilers of all useful knowledge, were familiar with the metaphysical speculations of the Hindus and Taoism is generally acknowledged to be a derivation of the ascetic philosophies of India. The principle dogma arising from the findings of the Annalists and Astrologers is evident throughout the Taoist conception. Astrology, alchemy and comparative metaphysics of a somewhat Vedantic conception underlie the more evident aspects of the Taoist doctrine.

The Chou dynasty was one of the warring periods in Chinese history. Strife and philosophy are incompatible, and Lao-Tze was most outspoken in his condemnation of the theory of war and aggression. At last growing weary with strife's of princes and the inconsistencies of society, Lao-Tze began to dream again of the peace that rests among the hills. After placing all of the responsibilities of his office in order, he pleaded for the privilege of retiring forever from the sight of men. This being granted, and his own age and infirmity being great, he mounted upon the back of his favorite ox and rode slowly away towards the boundaries which lie between China and the great mountains. He arrived at last at the gate of China, which leads to the Northwest. It was autumn when he reached the Hankow Pass and it was there that he met Yin Hsi, the keeper of the gate.

It appears that Yin Hsi was himself a great astrologer and mystic. At night he would spend many hours studying the motions of the stars and during one of these vigils he observed a strange body moving in the heavens, a light that rose over China and moved gradually Northwest to disappear among the distant peaks of the Himalayas. Yin Hsi turned to the ancient books and from them and his own meditation discovered that one of the greatest of living beings would shortly follow that route, passing the light itself along the road that led through the Hankow Pass. Yin Hsi therefore built himself a hut of grass by the side of the road and, seating himself in the doorway of the hut, waited for the coming of the Great Teacher.

Lao-tse. (*Sien-fo-tsi-tsoung.*)

At last, he observed approaching a great green ox and on its back a little old man, with white hair, wrapped in a great cloak. The heart of Yin Hsi beat rapidly within him. His inner eye perceived that this was the one for whom he waited. When Lao-Tze reached the hut of the gatekeeper Yin Hsi prostrated himself before the sage, beseeching him to remain a little while and instruct him in the secrets of Tao—the Way of Life. Lao-Tze acknowledged the request, and, being assisted to dismount from the ox, remained with the gatekeeper in his hut long enough to prepare his only literary work—the Tao Teh King. The manuscript was brief, consisting in all of five thousand characters. So condensed is the style, so abstract the terminology, that its profundity and scope are beyond the comprehension of the average reader.

Having completed his writing and presented it to Yin Hsi, Lao-Tze mounted the green ox again and passing through the gate continued alone and without provisions into the wild and desolate country that lay beyond. Beyond this point in the story, only fable remains. According to some accounts, he went forth to die; according to others, he journeyed to a mysterious valley where all the sages of the past dwelt together. Only this is known; that after his ninetieth year, he disappeared from China and was never heard from again.

His memory lived on, and while his sect never equaled that of Confucius in popularity, the little old white-haired man and his green ox wander forever up and down the roads of China, revisualized in each generation by pious Taoists. Nor was he ignored by the state. In the seventh century A. D. he was canonized by the reigning Tang Emperor, being lifted to the estate among the divine creatures of the world with the title The Great Supreme, the Emperor-God of the Dark First Cause. To this was afterwards added the further honor of being known simply and profoundly as the Ancient Master.

THE DOCTRINE OF TAOISM

The Tao Teh King is the foundation of the Taoist doctrine. The word Tao means loosely translated, the Way, the Bath, the Means, and even more, the Principle, the Truth or the Reality underlying all things. "Teh" means virtue, enlightenment, action performed in conformity with Principle. Thus, Tao Teh King means the Book of the Way of Virtue, or again the Book which reveals the code of spiritual conduct towards the Principle.

In spite of the unusual life of Lao-Tze and his extreme devotion to metaphysical speculations, his beliefs would probably not have survived had they been left without commentary and clarification. While Lao-Tze revealed the Principle, it remained for two great Chinese scholars, Lieh-tzu and Chuang-tzu, to elaborate and perfect the tradition and arrange its principles for world assimilation. It has been said of these men that they represent the highest standard of mystical scholarship in China. Lieh-tzu and Chuang-tzu lived about B.C. 400, and most of the Taoist texts which descend to this time have come through them rather than directly from Lao-Tze himself. Like their master, these fathers of Taoism lived obscure and simple lives so that little is known of the circumstances under which they promulgated Taoist dogma. Lieh-tzu seems to have lived in extreme poverty and Chuang-tzu, though he lived somewhat better, chose voluntary obscurity that his time might be free for meditation upon the mystery of the Principle. Therefore, when discussing Taoism, we cannot in every case divide between the master and these two ardent disciples. The three together are Taoism as far as its literary background is concerned. The pre-Taoist Annalists and Astrologers of Chou left no literary fragments relating to the doctrine.

The Taoist doctrine must be considered from both its theoretical and practical aspects. The theory of Taoism is summed up in the understanding of the nature of Tao or the Principle. The practical aspect is the simple or obscure method of living, and to both of these fundamentals were gradually added a complex structure of supernatural factors which, if not actually unknown to Lao-Tze himself, certainly find no emphasis in the Tao Teh King.

Tao, the Principle, must first be understood in all of its philosophical inferences. The Principle is the Absolute factor in existence. The Principle is termed Essence and it is described as self-existent, eternal, complete and infinite. It is the common quality from which all forms are externalized and into which they must ultimately return. The Principle neither grows nor diminishes for all forms into which it flows are extensions of itself, and there is never any actual separation to take place within it. The Principle is everywhere, and in one of the Taoist discourses the disciple refers to obscure places where the Principle may not be, but in each place the master assures him that the Principle is omnipresent, everywhere, always. The Principle is not only the ultimate extension of form into formlessness; it is also the ultimate extension of thought to an abstract, mindless origin. Intelligence, consciousness and force all retire into the Principle and become universalized through this retirement. The Principle is the only unqualified and unmodified factor in the universe. In the presence of the Principle the need for a world Sovereign or personal god ceases for the Taoist. The Principle possesses also the attribute of absolute Law in the sense that its very existence is the root of the plan and purpose for all existing creatures.

Lao-Tze acknowledges that it is impossible to understand the origin of the Principle, in fact he regards it as without origin, being absolutely eternal. "I do not know" said Lao-Tze, "from whom the Principle proceeded. It appears to have been before the Sovereign (God). It abounds and produces without replenishing itself. Incessantly overflowing, it does not empty itself. All beings have come forth from this Abyss, in which there is nothing." The Principle could not be termed exactly as germinal but it does possess the quality, in fact the infinite capacity, of producing forms, structures, types and kinds out of itself so that all things appear to proceed from nothing, to be sustained by nothing, and finally to fall back again or retire into nothing. But to Lao-Tze this seeming Nothing was in itself an all-inclusive root agency from which we get a paradox—all is nothing, nothing is all. Lao-Tze cannot explain why or how the Principle externalizes itself to become creation. Retiring into his own nature he is capable of accepting this fact as a transcendent truth. He further acknowledges that the Principle contains, identical with itself, certain intrinsic natures or conditions. The first of these is termed Te which is denominated the virtue of the Principle. We might say that a fact emanates a certain influence by the very virtue of it being a fact. This emanation is Te, and Te the virtue or energy in the Principle acts upon two other intrinsic modes which are called Yin and Yang. These last are referred to as the imminent properties of the Principle. Yin and Yang represent concentration and expansion. They are the father-mother attributes of deity, or of absolute energy, to be found in nearly all systems of metaphysical theology. Te, working upon Yin and Yang, causes the modes or properties to be externalized, whereupon Yang becomes heaven and Yin earth. By heaven and earth are not to be understood the invisible firmament or the terrestrial globe but rather diffusion and solidarity, or extension and limitation. These are the opposing factors through the mingling of which forms and organized entities are manifested. Yang, the principle of expansion, is in a sense identical with Tao itself. Yin, the principle of concentration or crystallization, being the apparent but unreal element in the phenomenon of creation.

To Lao-Tze the extremities Yin and Yang form an illusional manifestation in which all values are distorted and essential truths remain unperceived.

Unity, Tao, or the Principle, is the suspension of the opposites—the fact, the possession of which dissolves the illusion and releases consciousness from its bondage to the tyranny of good and evil.

Lao-Tze realized that when man resolved to destroy evil, he must also destroy good, for both of these are extremes counter-balancing each other, and to remove either destroys both. Therefore Lao-Tze substituted the Principle for both good and evil teaching that Tao, as the Cause of extremes, remained firm, unconditioned and unlimited by the forces which flowed from it. Tai-ding the extreme viewpoint that all phenomenal things arose from the chemistry of Yin and Yang, that is from struggle or striving or compounding, Lao-Tze rejected not only the world but the worlds of worldliness by which it is sustained and perpetuated. The moral inferences are inevitable. Man has two souls or super-substantial entities within him. The first is the body-soul, the anima or animating principle of form. This soul governs growth, health, bodily functions and such impulses and purposes as contribute to the bodily security. The other soul, super-substantially, is built up through life. One tradition says that this superior part is an inward condensation of a certain part of the breath; that when man inhales air into the lungs and exhales it again a certain small part remains each time and this small part condenses into the vehicle for the ethereal soul. It is this higher soul that survives the disintegration of the body at death. But all souls are ultimately absorbed into Tao. There is no final individual immortality. Taoism accepts the doctrine of Reincarnation as a means of explaining the cyclic course of the soul in its return to Tao or the Principle.

In essence Tao is extremely simple and, if it can be denuded of its superficialities, resembles very closely the philosophical speculations of Buddha. Taoism in practice becomes a philosophy of right use, of economy or resource, moderation of emotion, and all other reasonable courses of action which contribute to physical security and mental balance.

The practical aspects of Taoism arise naturally from the theoretical inferences. The person is to live as nearly as possible in Harmony with and like the Principle. Like the Principle he must be universal, like the Principle he must be impartial, like the Principle he must flow rhythmically through the phenomena of life. Like the Principle he must give without being less, he must gain without being more, and like the Principle he must achieve to his final liberation by becoming void of all qualities. As Lao-Tze says, "In imitation of the Principle, the sage allows beings to grow without impeding them, to live without monopolizing them, to act without exploiting them."

To live perfectly in harmony with the transcendent splendor of the Principle is to increase inwardly in understanding until the personality is completely liberated from all attachments and uncertainties. In Taoism, longevity is regarded as a virtue, not merely because of length of years but because when accomplished philosophically, it indicates supremacy over the self-destructive factors, at work in the conflict of life. Conservation must always be practiced. Waste is blasphemy. Excessive labor, emotional stress, over-study, worries, cares, responsibilities, ambitions—all these wear out the life and are contrary to the dictates of Tao. For the sage, effort must be without effort. The consciousness must flow from deed to deed and from thought to thought without confusion, complex, or dissension. Contact with humanity is wearing, the distress one sees is depressing, and until the sage is perfectly capable of perceiving the integrity behind all things, he should avoid all congested places that deplete and weary him. He should remain obscure, receiving only those worthy of his, consideration. He should never seep office or position because worldly promotion brings only illusionary honor and losses, forces which destroy the health and security.

Taoism is a belief limited to a certain class of mankind of natural mystical inclinations. Even to preach it is included among the wasted efforts. A man ready to understand the Principle becomes aware of it within himself. This awareness he cannot transfer to another, nor will discussion and argument bring as much good to the listener as it brings harm to the speaker. According to Taoism in its original form, there is no possibility of conversion in the ordinary sense of the word. You may talk to men forever, but they remain what they are—it is the one who talks who wears out. This being a fundamental verity, demonstrable in every walk of life, it is the duty of the sage to perfect the Law in himself. He will then be understood by those of similar mind and they are the only ones whose understanding is important. It is upon this point that Lao-Tze is supposed to have had his singular debate with Confucius. To Lao-Tze there was no family, no honor, no dignity and no achievement. To him, ceremony was a waste of words, prayer a waste of time, tradition a waste of thought, history a waste of writing. To Taoism there is neither past, present nor future, and in the illusional intervals that seem to be these things, nothing happens that is really important. Men die, other men are born; nations rise, other nations fall; philosophies rise and philosophies fall. Everything comes and goes, but none of this concerns the sage. His only real problem is his relationship with himself. The Taoist illustrates the principle of indifference in this way; a number of faggots grouped together make a fire; the flame having consumed one piece of wood passes on to another and the ashes that it leaves behind are of no importance, for only the flame itself that lives upon them all is real.

Lao-Tze recommended to live distantly from men that the illusions that arise from intimate intercourse with illusions might be avoided. He does not, however, demand such departure. He says: "To become a Taoist sage, it is not necessary to leave the world. Peace and purity can be obtained in the world." In Taoism, purity does not mean the practice of accepted social virtues necessarily. It rather means purity of a relationship with the inward realization. It means simplicity, detachment, a renunciation not accompanied by a sense of loss.

The doctrines of Tao include an important understanding of the word or thought of lowliness. If a man lifts himself to a high place, everything flows away from him. If he makes of himself a low place, everything flows into him. Therefore, the doctrine recommends that the consciousness of the Taoist should be like the sea which fills the lowest places of the earth, inscrutable and unknown, into which all the rivers of the earth pour their waters—but the sea is never full. If a Taoist is placed over other men, his power should never be felt. He should rule with gentleness. As Lao-Tze says, "It is not by oppressing man but by serving man that we conquer man."

The sage should perform all virtuous actions. At the same time, it is hypocrisy not to realize that by so doing, he helps himself most. A man who does right in the hope of heaven is not an honest man but a self-seeking man, and whenever one humbles himself in the hope of gaining some great ultimate reward, that is selfishness and might fust as well be acknowledged as such. The true sage is incapable of egotism because it is a destructive emotion leading to vainglorious thought and action, and consequently leads away from Tao. Lao-Tze views ambition as one of the greatest of the cardinal sins. Of him it may be truly said that he taught "the path of glory leads but to the grave." Men but wear themselves out trying to please others. Nothing pleases others and nothing pleases themselves. The doing of the necessary is virtue; the doing of the unnecessary is vice.

In the Taoist doctrines, there are two forms of goodness—collective and individual. Collective goodness partakes of Tao, for the Principle sustains all things impartially. Individual good partakes of ignorance for individuality itself is an illusion. It would be incorrect to say that Lao-Tze taught men to be cruel and indifferent to each other, but he certainly did advise that we not sustain the errors of others through sympathy or condolence. As it is always unpopular to tell the truth and few desire to know the facts about their own lives and thoughts, Lao-Tze again recommended that the true sage remain in so obscure a position that his advice would not lively be sought. Let those who desire knowledge go to those who claim to possess it. Taoism is not founded upon knowledge; it is founded upon the distinct realization that the empty cup is the most useful one. For this reason, Lao-Tze condemned Confucius for studying, intimating that wisdom comes from within and foolishness out of books. This may be an extreme viewpoint, for Lao Tze was nearly eighty years old and extremely set at the time of the debate. The principle involved warns the individual against intellectualism as a substitute for inner experience. We have the proof today and the fact that the thoroughly schooled man may not be an educated man and again an educated man may not be a wise man.

Lao-Tze was born in one of the most conventional, law-ridden, tradition-bound countries of the world. Birth, life and death were circumscribed by ceremonials. Every element of the social system was venerated without understanding and worshipped without an inner vision. It is not surprising, then, that the master reasoned thus concerning laws; "Men invent laws because they cannot longer perceive the Law. They invent virtues when the Sovereign Virtue is obscure. Ceremony and tradition take the place of man's incapacity to sense the original inner equity and frankness of relationship." He also adds that the invention of politics was the beginning of all abuses. To Lao-Tze, the idea of men governing each other was ridiculous in a state of social consciousness where no man was capable of governing himself. He laid the foundations of the social psychology in which enlightenment would finally make government an evident absurdity. Under Tao, all men live the Law and until men live the one Law, there can be nothing but lawlessness among men. Great laws come from the Principle, small laws come from governments and princes. Even if a prince be perfectly just, even if he be wiser than all other mortals, still he cannot make laws that are real or permanent. Laws do not come from man but Tao, the Principle, as Law comes through men who have discovered it and have identified their inner lives with its purposes. Thus Lao-Tze attacks the very foundations of the state. He shows the ridiculousness of the pomp and ceremony with which men fool each other and too often themselves. Why should men make laws when the universe has established immutable decrees which nothing can withstand? If men must follow laws, they must follow the laws of nature, for these laws represent the Principle flowing through the forms which make up the world.

THE DISCIPLINES OF TAOISM

Lao-Tze practiced and advocated two forms of metaphysical self-control: the control of breath and the control of action. The archives of the Third Ministry probably supplied the technique of breath control, which had long been practiced in India. Respiration was brought more and more completely under the control of will, with the result that it caused an ecstatic state to arise in the body chemistry. The simple breath control was later elaborated into a complex system of exercises borrowed from the Buddhist and Yogi schools. By the control of respiration and by directing the inhaled breath throughout the body by a peculiar mental discipline, the nature is not only purified but rendered placid and relaxed. The complete bodily silence resulting from the breath technique released the superior consciousness for its consummation with Tao.

There is only one direct reference in the actual words of Lao-Tze to ecstasy, but it indicates definitely the use of the Hindu exercises and formulas. Lao-Tze recognized the mystical experience and taught the at-one-ment with Cause by forcing the cessation of conflict among the elements of external personality.

The control of action was a distinct feature of the Taoist cult. One does everything by doing nothing, one goes everywhere by staying still. All outward action interferes with the transcendent personality, the universal Self which experiences all things inwardly. The Principle, if philosophically understood, would result in a brilliant internal experience, but as most men are incapable of perceiving metaphysical subtleties, the Taoist doctrines would have a very detrimental effect upon the unlearned in mystical matters.

Lao-Tze denied religious organizations, discouraged and disparaged priestcraft's, ignored rituals and formulas, and had nothing good to say for that enthusiasm to convert, present in most religious systems. For this reason, the outer growth of his doctrine was paralyzed from the very first. Those who possessed it remained silent, and obeying the precepts of their master did nothing as social forces towards enlightenment. Lao-Tze left no pattern for the furtherance of his beliefs, and the doctrine came finally to be entirely dependent for its continuity upon the beliefs and capacities of those who affirmed it.

Tao was the goal, and many were the means that men devised in their efforts to achieve the Principle. The doctrine of inaction, taken with all the force of its literal inference, resulted in the Taoism of today, a complex of divergent factors.

Lao-Tze's teaching of inaction was founded upon the spiritual truth that inner experience is the one reality of life and men whose minds are focused upon outward experience divide themselves from Truth by the very emphasis which they place upon the theory of outward accomplishment. Lao-Tze's inaction was really detachment, man releasing himself from the auto-hypnosis of the things he does, to emphasize the profound truth of what he is. Taoism of today is not the doctrine as given by Lao-Tze. The modern cult has been heavily influenced by Buddhism and the indigenous spirit worship of the Chinese. It now has priests and temples and shrines and altars, and a triad of divinities centering around the deified personality of Lao-tzu himself. The simple, austere doctrine of the Obscure Sage has become a fantastic body of beliefs in which genii of every order impose their influence upon the fate of mortals.

QUOTATIONS

A few extracts from the Tao-Teh-King give us a general insight into the mind of the Sage himself and the abstruse quality of his original teachings:

"He who would gain a knowledge of the nature and attributes of the nameless, undefinable God (Tao) must first set himself free from all earthly desires."

"The highest excellence is like that of water. The excellence of water appears in it benefiting all things, and in its occupying, without striving to the contrary, the low place which all men dislike."

"When the work's done, and one's name is becoming distinguished, to withdraw into obscurity is the way of heaven."

"When one gives undivided attention to the vital breath, and brings it to the utmost degree of pliancy, he can become as a tender babe. When he has cleansed away the most mysterious sights of his imagination, he can become without a flaw."

"The state of vacancy should be brought to the utmost degree, and that of stillness guarded with unwearyingly vigor."

"He (the sage) is free from self-display, and therefore he shines; from self-assertion, and therefore he is distinguished; from self-boasting, and therefore his merit is acknowledged; from self-complacency, and therefore, he acquires superiority. It is because he is thus free from striving that therefore no one in the world is able to strive with him."

"Man takes his law from the earth; the earth takes its law from heaven; heaven takes its law from the Tao."

"He who knows other men is discerning; he who knows himself is intelligent. He who overcomes others is strong; he who overcomes himself is mighty."

"There is no guilt greater than to sanction ambition; no calamity greater than to be discontented with one's lot."

"The perception of what is small is the secret of clear-sighted ness."

"Governing a great state is like cooking small fish." (Small fish are easily overcooked.)

"But I have three precious things which I prize and hold vast. The first is gentleness; the second is economy; and the third is shrinking from taking precedence of others."

"It is the Way of Heaven to diminish superabundance, and to supplement deficiency. It is not so with the way of man. He takes away from those who have nothing to add to his own superabundance."

Yours sincerely,

Manly P. Hall

NOTICE—Your subscription to the Monthly Letter expired with the April issue. Please send us your renewal if you wish the New Series. If you have renewed kindly disregard this notice. Renewed $1.00

JUNE 15, 1936

Dear Friend,

CONFUCIUS

Shuh-liang-Heih was a doughty warrior whose ancestry went back to the Imperial family of Shang. His exploits of great strength and courage have become part of the heroic tradition in China. As Shuh-liang-Heih felt the weight of years descending upon him, he became gravely conscious of the misfortune in his domestic life. There would be no son to perform the ancestral rites to his memory. His wife had given him nine daughters and this tragedy so preyed upon the mind of the aged soldier that he decided to divorce his unfortunate spouse and take a new wife in his closing years.

With due ceremony and the full practice of the elegancies of the day, he approached the ancient and illustrious family of Yen where three marriageable daughters of exceptional virtue and beauty were awaiting husbands. It was a delicate matter due to the great discrepancy in age. The Lord of Yen, with a gesture most unusual to the gravity of Chinese etiquette, discussed the problem frankly with the three young women. He pointed out the deplorable disaster which oppressed the soul of Shuh-liang-Heih; he assured his daughters that the old warrior was of most excellent ancestry, and desired of them that they should come to their own decision as to desirability of such a match.

The youngest daughter, Ching-Tsai, realizing that her father desired the alliance, immediately offered herself. Thus, it came to pass that Shuh-liang-Heih in his seventieth year took to wife the seventeen-year-old daughter of the house of Yen.

Ching-Tsai was fully aware of the real purpose of the marriage, and being of deeply religious spirit besought the gods and genii for their aid that a son might be born to venerate his father's memory. There was a sacred mountain not far distant and to this holy place she made frequent pilgrimage. It was on one of these pious journeys that a curious vision came to Ching-Tsai. Five ancient and mysterious sages appeared to the expectant mother as in a dream, leading in their midst a strange animal. The creature was about the size and shape of a small cow, some say a lion, but it was covered with scales like a dragon and carried a single horn in the middle of its forehead. The Ki-lin is a metaphysical and symbolical animal which only appeared when some great enlightenment was to be conferred upon mankind. In its mouth the Ki-lin carried a tablet of jade, which it dropped at the feet of Ching-Tsai. Upon the tablet were the words: "A child as pure as crystal shall be born when the Chou are on their decline. He will be a king, but without any dominions." The five sages then spoke, declaring that the coming child would be wise beyond all mortals and that all of his descendants would honor him as their most illustrious ancestor. The sages then bade the mother tie a piece of cloth to the horn of the sacred animal, which she did, whereupon the whole vision disappeared.

Many miraculous circumstances attended the birth of the predestined child. All through the night, two dragons crouched on the roof of Shuh-liang-Heih's house. Heavenly musicians filled the air with sacred chanting, and five mysterious old men kept entering and leaving the birth chamber. The celestial choir kept chanting, "All heaven rejoices at the birth of this holy child." And so, in the fall months of the year B.C. 551, a little son was born to Ching-Tsai. According to the Chinese tradition "on the body of the infant were forty-nine marks of his future greatness and on his breast were visible the words, he will point out, he will act, he will decide, he will accomplish the times." The five old men were supposed to be Eu-hi, and the four patriarch-emperors. Together they are called the Ti. Thus, in a land of mystery, amidst circumstances exceeding strange, there came into the world the philosopher K'ung-fu-tsu (words Latinized into Confucius), the Perfect Sage, the Ancient and Illustrious Teacher, the Superior Man, posthumously created by Duke of Ne, and the uncrowned Emperor of China.

When Confucius was but three years of age, his father died and the young mother dedicated her life to the care and education of her mysterious little son. It is beyond question that her continual guidance and the purity of her personal life did much to mold the character of her child. Throughout life he exhibited a certain traditional gravity which is traceable directly to Ching-tsai's tradition-bound influence. Little is known concerning the boyhood of Confucius other than the traditional report that from his earliest years, he exhibited extraordinary intellectual powers. He came into this life with an infinite capacity to learn and applied himself so successfully to the arts of self-improvement that at seventeen he had already entered upon a public life. His serious and studious mind at an early age concerned itself with the political and sociological aspects of Chinese life. The unusual depth of his learning is attested by the account current throughout China that of all those who took the celebrated examinations of the Classics, Confucius alone passed all the elaborate tests with a grade of one hundred percent. Confucius was married at the age of nineteen, but after many years separated from his wife for reasons unrecorded. One son graced their union, but he died before his father.

The rise of Confucius in the political system of his day can be summed up as follows: he was first made superintendent of the Granaries of the Marquis of Lu (now Shantung). Later, the pasture lands of the state also came under his control. In his fiftieth year, he was elevated to the estate of Prefect. A year later he was further promoted to Chief Judge, and three years after this came to his highest political position—Vice Minister of the Earldom of Lu.

During these various periods of life, the actions of Confucius were marked by a severity of mien and an uncompromising devotion to honesty. A man of his unswerving devotion to integrity could scarcely hope for high office during a period as degenerate and corrupt politically as that of the declining Chou. The Earldom of Lu flourished under his care, becoming so rich and prosperous that intriguers from other provinces, jealous and fearful, organized to destroy the growing power of the Confucian policy.

Confucius apparently never entirely recovered from the disillusionment of his political years. He saw men, intentionally corrupt, undermining the integrity of the state for their own profit. He beheld a general decadence in ethics and law. To him, this decline represented the collapse of all that was fine and noble in the Chinese order of existence. As early as his twenty-second year, being then but three years in public office, Confucius began to perceive the hopelessness of coping politically with the corruption of the state. The spirit of the reformer being strongly within him, he realized that many evils must be overcome before law itself as a regulator of human affairs could function honestly. It may be contended that the viewpoint of Confucius was too narrow and that many of his trials were of his own making, but history records him as a rather versatile person who combined strength of mind with strength of body, and in the arts was a polished performer upon the lute. His ability as a charioteer is especially noted, his skill with horses bringing him much fame. Whatever he did, he accomplished whole-heartedly and sincerity of effort marked his every action. His mind was thorough and orderly, yet not entirely free from a certain bitterness, especially in advancing years. He suffered, as all idealists must suffer. He was so thoroughly equipped intellectually to help China that he was never able to understand fully why China refused his help. Whenever his program was attempted, it succeeded, but it seemed as though no one wanted his program. Intrigues destroyed vision. The state was a chaos of petty evils, and philosophy found small favor in the sight of princes.

Confucius was Vice Minister of Lu for a short time when, with the certainty of a man who has thought all things through, he arose one day and closing the doors of state behind him, and leaving princes to their numerous quarrels, took up a life of wandering which extended over a period of thirteen years. This period in the life of the Master was devoted to two specific purposes. He offered himself and his advices to the various feudal states in an effort to accomplish necessary reforms. He also gathered about him disciples and followers to whom he preached his ideas and in whom he implanted doctrines and ideals that were later to change the whole civilization of Cathay.

After these thirteen years of teaching and preaching, of offering and being repulsed, Confucius returned at the age of sixty-seven to his own state of Lu, wiser from the experiences of his wanderings. He never resumed a political career, but established a school where he taught his Utopian vision to a considerable number of disciples. Tradition tells that the total number of his scholars exceeded three thousand and of this group seventy-two so excelled in sagacity and penetration that he regarded them as actual disciples participating with him in the dream of the coming age.

Confucius lived during one of the most important transition periods in the history of human society. Contemporary with him was not only Lao-tzu in China, but Gautama Buddha in India, Zarathustra Spitama in Persia, and Pythagoras in Greece. Confucius was forced to stand by and watch the decay of culture, form, tradition and ceremony. Men no longer studied the Odes and the Annals. They no longer performed the rites. All that seemed beautiful and fine to Confucius was sacrificed to avarice and dissension. Confucius therefore appointed himself a perpetuator and preserver of the ancient order of society. He re-edited, revised and reformed, compiling together what he believed to be the spirit of Chinese culture performing in this way a task, more vital than he was ever to know.

About two hundred years before the Christian era, the libraries of China were destroyed by Imperial edict and had it not been for Confucius, the antiquity of Chinese thought would have almost entirely perished. With years already heavy upon him, his whole nature melancholy with a deep sadness, the sadness of one who understands but cannot act, Confucius wrote on, striving to preserve, trying to make some contribution that would be of permanent good to the people of China.

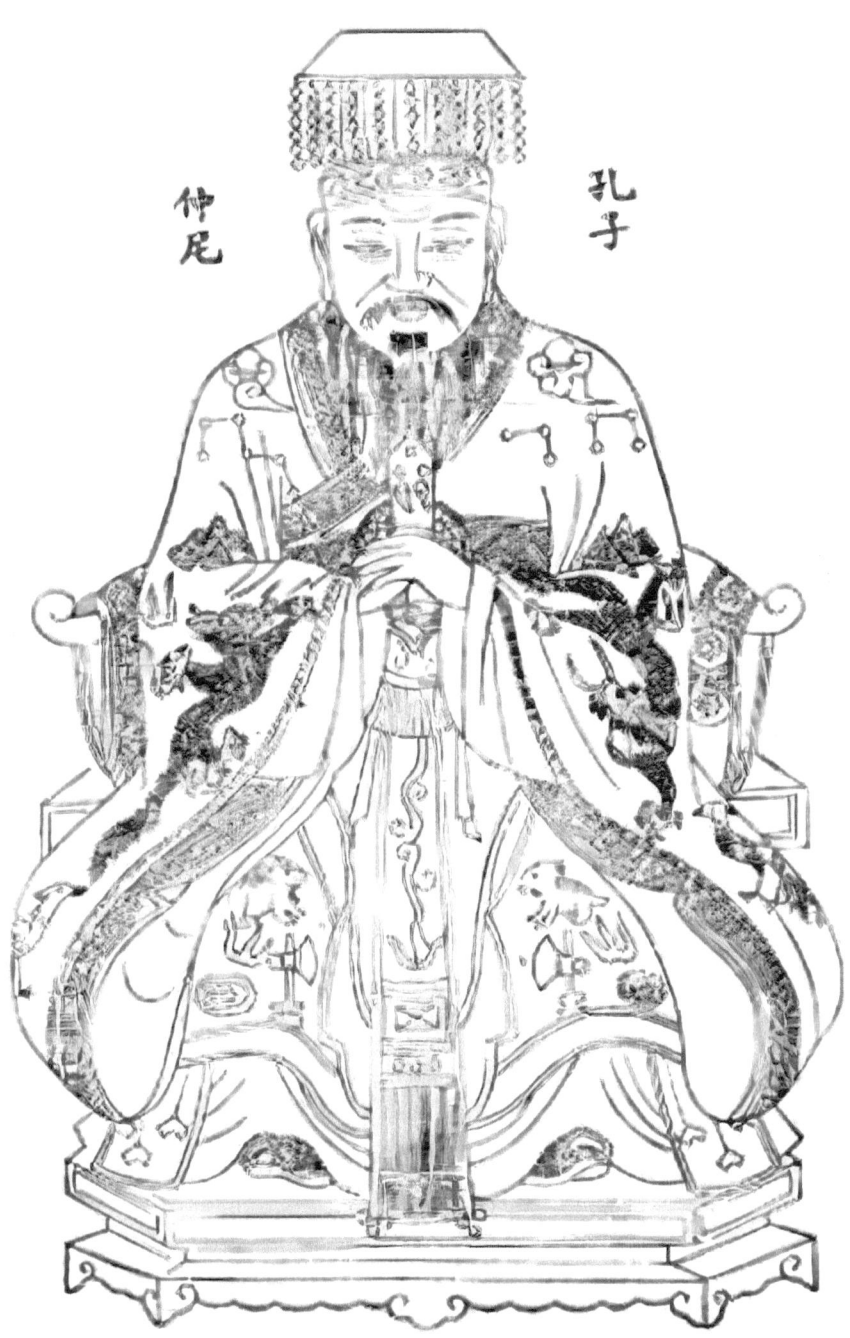

CONFUCIUS

It was in the closing years of his life that Confucius contacted, or possibly more correctly came to understand, the oldest and strangest book in China—the Yih-King [I Ching], the Classic of Change. Even in the sixth century B.C. the authorship of the Yih-King was obscure. It emerged with China itself from the dark periods before history. Some modern scholars have even declared that the Yih-King is the oldest book in the world. Commentaries had been written to this work before Confucius, but none of them seemed entirely satisfactory to the organized mind of the Superior Man. So, he prepared himself an elaborate commentary which commends him definitely to a belief in divination and magic. Possibly his interview with Lao-tze influenced this commentary, although many years had passed since Confucius had paid that memorable visit to the librarian of the Third Ministry.

Death came to Confucius while he was still engrossed in his literary endeavors. The last part of his life was divided between teaching and editing the Chronicle of the Earldom of Lu. In B.C. 479 Confucius announced, in the strange terminology to which he was so much addicted, that "the sacred mountain was about to fall, that the ridge beam was about to break, that the sage was about to take his departure."

A short time before the passing of the Master, a huntsman in the forest of Lu slew a strange monster. He brought the body of the creature into the town to be exhibited to the amazed populace. It was an animal the size of a cow covered with scales and armed with a single horn. Upon beholding it, Confucius declared that its death denoted his own passing. It was the Ki-lin, the peculiar animal of wisdom, and its destruction marked the close of the period of enlightenment.

It was soon after this that Confucius took to his couch. His last words are variously recorded, but in substance they are the same: "No wise sovereign arises. There is none in the Empire who will make me his master. My time has come to die." Another version reads: "Since no prince of this time has enough intelligence to understand me, it is better then I die, for my plans will not materialize." After these words Confucius did not speak again, but, remaining silent on his couch for six days, departed on the seventh, in his seventy-third year, surrounded by his disciples. He was buried outside of the capital city of Lu, where his tomb remains to this day. Thus ended the quest of the Superior Man who spent a life-time searching for an honest ruler.

THE DOCTRINES OF CONFUCIUS

The principal source of the Confucian doctrines is the analects, in Chinese the lun yu. Strictly speaking, this work was not written by the Master but is rather a collection of his opinions, interspersed with the words of other teachers and scholars, and also anecdote material. The statements directly contributed to Confucius are generally preceded by the statement "the Master said" or "the Master answered." The scope and quality of Confucius' mind may be more fully appreciated from the choice which he made from the ancient Odes and Annals in his editorial capacity of preserver and restorer.

Confucius was not a mystic, although he showed no aversion to mystical speculation, and occasionally indulged in it. His mind was devoted to practical problems concerned with the social and political survival of the Chinese Empire. A devoutly religious man, he refrained from any direct effort to expound theological opinions. Under the general term "heaven" he summarized the spiritual and causal factors which animate and direct material creatures. The decrees of Heaven are absolute and immutable. All things subsist and survive according to the ordinances of heaven. Beyond this point, he seldom ventured, leaving metaphysical speculations to men more given to abstractions.

The Master clung to ancient orders of thought and action because to him, they represented the Will of Heaven. Acknowledging that customs had decayed, it seemed to him that the waning of the virtues paralleled the failure of the rites and ceremonies which had been given to China by the first illumined messengers of Heaven. Confucius attributed to the universe a mental viewpoint actually and intrinsically his own. To him, the reasonable and the evident and the virtuous must be the will of heaven.

The central thought of Confucianism may be summed up in the simple premise that the wisdom of the past sustains the virtue of the present, and the virtue of the present insures the well-being of the future. Like Socrates, Confucius affirmed that if it is possible to cure the disease of irrationality with which men are afflicted, the permanence of all desirable conditions is assured. Nations, being but aggregates of individuals, express collectively those attitudes which persons express individually. Divine orders of beings reveal to those who are observing certain standards of thought and action, the rites, customs and modes which have been established by the Will of Heaven in all the departments of nature. If men will heed the examples which the universe sets forth, they can bring into manifestation that perfection which exists everywhere as a potentiality.

Confucius felt himself called to the task of accomplishing a practical reconstruction of human standards of ethics. He dreamed of the Golden Age or ideal state, a day when all evil and dissension should pass away, and truth become supreme. Of this dream the Master said: "When the Great Principle prevails, the whole world becomes a republic; they elect men of talent, virtue and ability; they tall; about sincere agreement and cultivate universal peace. A competent provision is secured for the aged until their death; employment for the middle ages, and the means of growing up for the young. Bach man has his own rights and each woman her individuality safe-guarded." This one vision places Confucius among the great idealists of the world. Men of this later age dream as he dreamed and the dream still waits fulfillment.

The Confucian dream of the New Age is entirely consistent with the Platonic ideal of rulership by the philosophic elect. The first step towards the achievement of this glorious state was, according to Confucius, the development of the Superior Man, one in whom the knowledge of virtue is perfect and who lives in harmony with that knowledge. We therefore find set forth in the words attributed to Confucius those qualities which are necessary to the achievement of a collective state of security. The Master said: "The Superior Man seeks in himself, whereas ordinary men seek in others for truth. The object of the Superior Man is truth—truth achieved through consistency with the highest standards of the common good and a strict application of the Principle." In another place, Confucius said: "The practice of right living is deemed the highest practice."

In affairs of the state Confucius maintained that in all things the wise must rule and the unlearned obey. However, he also desired to universalize educational opportunity so that ignorance would become a matter of choice rather than of necessity. One of the disciples of the Master said that if he were made Prime Minister of China, he could insure the country peace sufficient for a thousand years by means of the Confucian code.

Confucius accepted the continuity of life after death, saying: "that the bones and flesh should return to earth is what is appointed, but the soul in its energy can go everywhere." He discouraged, however, intercourse between men and spirits, saying that it was an unrighteous act to weary the departed.

In his own day, Confucius was regarded as a man of very conservative viewpoints because he believed in the perpetuation of the niceties and gentilities of human relationship. He warned against intimacies and all actions which had a disparaging effect upon the opinions and conducts of man. He realized that the failure of little courtesies and small elegancies and the beauties of human relationship presaged the end of civilization. To Confucius progress was measured by the intrinsic fineness which distinguished the Superior Man. The Master himself was a man of extremely simple tastes, who utterly disliked ostentation and the false assumption of grandeur in any of its forms, who delighted in little formalities which bespoke courtesy and grace. Ritual and tradition as roots of hypocrisy he abhorred, but he envisioned the Superior Man as possessing a gentle, natural dignity, preserving respect and honor. The life of Confucius exemplified his belief in the magnificence of little things. Michael Angelo sounded a Confucian keynote when he said: "Trifles make perfection, and perfection is no trifle." The failure of little things, of subtle forces, of beautiful traditions, must inevitably bring great enterprises down to ruin.

In spite of his courtly consciousness, Confucius was neither arrogant nor self-sufficient. If his words produced meritorious results, he took no credit to himself. If he failed, he did not accept the blame, stating repeatedly that success and failure are according to the Will of Heaven. On one occasion, he was told that men did not understand him and he replied that it was no affliction not to be understood by men, but rather an affliction not to understand men.

In the analects he sums up the course of his own life: "When I attained the age of fifteen, I became bent upon study. At thirty, I was a confirmed student. At forty, nought could move me from my course. At fifty, I comprehended the Will and decrees of Heaven. At sixty, my ears were attuned to them. At seventy, I could follow my heart's desire without overstepping the lines of rectitude."

To the degree that Lao-tze depreciated all human knowledge, Confucius admired and cultivated the arts and sciences. He sought union with Universal Truth, not in the ascetic way of inward silence, but by the scholar's path of self-improvement. Taoism teaches that by achieving the One we know all. Confucianism teaches that by knowing all we discover the One. The Confucian path may be summarized in the words of the Master himself:

"Concentrate the mind upon the Good Way. Maintain firm hold upon virtue. Rely upon philanthropy. Find recreation in the arts. And never withhold instruction from any man."

CONFUCIAN DISCIPLINES

Confucius did not promulgate metaphysical disciplines among his disciples. It does not appear that he either indulged in or taught the meditative and contemplative practices that had been introduced to the Chinese mind by teachers and pilgrims from India. Confucius was too thoroughly Chinese to borrow the philosophies of other people. The fragments that have descended from the original Confucism school indicate that virtue and knowledge were the fundamentals of the master's teachings. Virtue was interpreted Socratically as right conduct, and knowledge, much in the thought of Lord Bacon, as the achievement of all things knowable. Virtue and knowledge reacted upon each other. Virtue increased the capacity for knowledge, and knowledge supplied the elements from which the standard of virtue was compounded. Live well, study diligently, and apply all knowledge to its useful ends. This, in substance, was the Confucian concept of right and truth.

The disciples of the master imposed certain disciplines upon themselves. They moderated the extremes of their emotions, reformed the excesses of their outward lives, and cleansed the mind of its inconstancies and its inconsistencies. They further cultivated gravity of deportment and faithfulness in small matters. They detached their minds from thoughts of rewards, being satisfied to labor and to learn without other reward than the improvement that they wrought within themselves. The Confucian philosophy is particularly applicable to our modern world because of the intensely practical emphasis that pervades and dominates the entire system. With wisdom, the end and virtue the means, the course of life was clarified, and the mind freed from the distress of conflicting opinions of schoolmen and the obstinate absurdities of theologians.

Confucius was not deceived by any vain optimism within himself. As a youth he dreamed greatly but as a mature man he realized that hundreds of thousands of years must pass before virtue and wisdom will rule the human race. He taught not a glamorous doctrine suitable for immature and inconstant mortals. Rather, he set down certain immutable truths which men might accept or reject at will. Neither acceptance nor rejection could in any way affect the intrinsic nature of the facts themselves. Men live not merely to barter and exchange for a little time, or to spend their years in idle or unfruitful courses, but rather to accomplish virtue and achieve wisdom. Man is truly human to the degree that he is truly good and truly wise. Not wealth nor power, nor authority, nor high birth are the proper objects of admiration. Only the wise man is truly admirable, only the virtuous man is worthy of respect. The

Confucian discipline is consequently the accomplishment of self-improvement, the dedication of the life throughout all its years to noble motive and high purpose. From childhood on, nobility must be cultivated. Nobility is gentleness, unselfishness, prudence, tolerance, temperance, and most of all a constant fixing of the mind upon the attributes of true greatness. In low office a man must be faithful, in high office he must be just, in all his transactions he must be honest, and in all things throughout his days he must value his honor above all gain and his character above compromise.

This might not sound like a metaphysical discipline, yet the achievement of the Confucian code is by no means easy. Men may pray for a few moments each day or meditate for a little time upon some high resolve. But to live well all of the time simply because right living is man's first duty to himself and others—this tests the courage and devotion of even the strongest. What a noble world this would be if all men were honest; yet honesty, so small a word and so simple a matter, is difficult beyond words. Peace is easier than war, honesty simpler than intrigue, wisdom more natural than ignorance, but the world chooses the less noble course and only a few among men practice those simple virtues which are the very essence of human relationship.

To Confucius, the fundamental facts of life were evident. He lived them more nobly than most men. He taught them with a devotion that has brought him the respect of the whole world. Confucius belongs not to Cathay but to all of mankind. His message, continuing through the centuries, descends after twenty-five hundred years as real and as practical as it was in his own day. Would that Confucius could live today and preach honesty and honor to the men of this generation which needs him as sorely as did ancient China. But if he stood upon the street corners of our cities, he would suffer again the ill fortunes that he met before. A few would follow him as of old, but even today it is unlikely that there would be governors who would listen, or princes to make him their minister, or a king to harken to his doctrines. Honesty and honor have little place today in the course of empire. Yet sometime, in a future better than the present, the world will remember the Superior Man who gave to China the life of wisdom.

After the passing of Confucius, the principal exponent of his doctrine was the philosopher Mencius who was born B.C. 372 and died about B.C. 289. Like Confucius, Mencius lived a quiet and obscure life. Centuries after his death he was canonized with Confucius and in the popular veneration of China holds a position second only to his master as an exponent of the doctrines of virtue and wisdom.

QUOTATIONS

A few extracts from the analects are representative of the profundity and nobility of Confucius' mind.

"Do not unto any man that which thou wouldst not he should do unto you."

"People despotically governed and kept in order by punishments may avoid infraction of the law, but they will lose their moral sense."

"The people can be made to follow a certain path, but they cannot be made to know the reason why."

"If a country had none but good rulers for a hundred years, crime might be stamped out and the death-penalty abolished."

"The higher type of man is one who acts before he speaks, and professes only what he practices."

"A man without charity in his heart—what has he to do with ceremonies? A man without charity in his heart—what has he to do with music."

"Is not he a sage who neither anticipates deceit nor suspects bad faith in others, yet is prompt to detect them when they appear?"

When a man asked Confucius concerning the principle of returning good for evil, the master replied:

"What, then, is to be the return for good? Rather should you return justice for injustice and good for good."

"My function is to indicate rather than to originate."

"If I am walking with two other men, each of them will serve as my teacher. I will pick out the good points of the one and imitate them, and the bad points of the other and correct them in myself."

"To divine wisdom and perfect virtue, I can lay no claim. All that can be said of me is that I never falter in the course which I pursue and am unwearyingly in my instruction of others."

"I used to spend whole days without food and whole nights without sleep in order to meditate. But I made no progress. Study, I found, was better."

"Study without thought is vain; thought without study is perilous."

"Having heard the True Way in the morning, what matters it if one should come to die at night?"

"The scholar who is bent on studying the principles of virtue, yet is ashamed of bad clothes and coarse food, is not yet fit to receive instruction."

"Virtue cannot live in solitude: neighbors are sure to grow up around it."

"It is bootless to discuss accomplished facts, to protest against things past remedy, to find fault with things bygone."

"It is not easy to find a man who, after three years of self-cultivation, has not reached happiness."

"Two classes of men never change: the wisest of the wise and the dullest of the dull."

Sincerely yours,

Manly P. Hall

JULY 15, 1936

Dear Friend,

BUDDHA

In the Tushita heaven, a realm of blissful realization, far beyond the sphere of mortal thinking, there dwelt a luminous and enlightened Sattva or being, by name Prabhapala. The inward perception of this purified and perfected Self perceived that but one incarnation remained to be accomplished among men before the law of Karma was fulfilled by the Nirvana. Prabhapala then enquired of the Law the circumstances of his final incarnation, and having perfected his inward perception of the conditions through which he should pass, announced: "I am going to be reincarnated in the family of King Suddhodana. I will renounce the royal dignity, leave the world, preach the Law, and procure the salvation of mortals and immortals."

King Suddhodana ruled a province north of Benares including a considerable part of what is now called Nepal. The chief city of the district was Kapilavastu and here were the palaces of the reigning house. King Suddhodana had married two sisters, daughters of the neighboring clan of Koli. The sisters' names were Maya and Frajapati and although both were childless, they continued in the kingly favor, the favorites of his household.

It can well be understood therefore that great happiness was in the land of the Sakyas when word came forth that the elder sister, then in her forty-fifth year, was to have a child. Maya, or as she is frequently termed Mahamaya, alone knew the secret of the destiny she bore. Surrounded by a great splendor of light and accompanied by the songs of the Devas, Prabhapala descended with the glory of the noonday sun from the Tushita heaven to take upon himself an earthly form. According to the old records, the conception took place at the 8th day of the 4th Moon at the moment of the rising of Venus. Maya perceived in a vision at this time an elephant with six tusks which, descending upon a path of light, entered into her side. She described the strange occurrence to Suddhodana who immediately summoned the wisest of the Brahmins. These astrologer-sages, after examining into the whole circumstances, reported to the king: "A great sage is to be born. If he does not retire into a holy life, he will become kings of the whole world."

There are several accounts of the birth of Gautama Siddhartha, but they agree that the child was born out of doors under a tree. In one account, Maya was journeying to the house of her parents. According to another, she partook herself to one of the parks in the palace grounds. It was again the 8th day of the 4th Moon and again Venus was rising. Maya came to the Sala tree, the low-hanging branches of which were heavy with beautiful flowers. As she lifted up her hand to pluck a branch from the tree, the Buddha was born from her right side without pain. Indra, god of the air, received the Divine Child and celestial beings, caused streams of heavenly water to flow upon the newborn babe. After the heavenly beings had propitiated the Perfect Incarnation, the infant Buddha stepped down upon the ground and took seven steps to each of the four corners of the world and with a clear voice stated his mission. A lotus flower sprang up at the four extremities of his steps. The infant then returned to the arms of Indra, becoming thereafter an entirely normal baby.

Maya, the mother of the Enlightened One, died on the seventh day after the birth of her child, for it was written in the ancient law that the mothers of perfected souls should not survive beyond the seventh day. The infant prince was thereafter entrusted to the care of his aunt Prajapati who in every way fulfilled the duties of a mother. The Divine Child was named Prince Siddhartha. Brahmin priests came to the court of King Suddhodana to predict the future of his newborn son and heir. Among the pilgrims came Asita, the holy man who dwelt alone in the distant mountains. He fell in adoration before the infant prince, discovering on the body of the babe the thirty-two marks of wisdom and the eighty secondary significators of divinity. After completing his examination of the little prince, Asita wept, declaring that Perfect Enlightenment was born into the world but that he, the pilgrim monk, Asita, should not live to hear the preaching of the Enlightened.

King Suddhodana learned from his astrologers that his little son was destined to be no ordinary man. Two careers were possible for the prince. He could become the greatest king in Asia, extending his rule to the furthest corners of the Eastern world, or he could become a priest, the greatest priest who ever lived, master of the inner empire of the eternal Self. The king was troubled. He feared his son might chance to be a priest. To prevent Siddartha from choosing the ascetic's life, the king surrounded him with all the luxuries and inducements of wealth and power. The prince had palaces all his own and vast gardens filled with the most beautiful plants and flowers. There were lakes with shining fish and little boats. There was music and all the enticements that could be conceived and executed with Eastern lavishness. In this world of beauty and superficial charm, the prince was prevented from seeing any of the sickness, sordidness and misery of the poor man's lot.

Prince Siddhartha was given the beautiful Yasodhara in marriage. The king of Kapilavastu was now satisfied that he had set his son upon the road to conquest. Rich, happy, entirely ignorant of the evils which beset the average mortal, the prince was now secure, and it seemed impossible that anything could turn him to the ascetic's path. But king Suddhodana had not reckoned with the powers of those celestial beings who were watching from their high heavens. One day while the prince was riding in the gardens of his palace the sages abiding in the Tushita heaven sent a vision which took the form of an aged man, stumbling along, leaning upon a heavy staff. Prince Siddhartha gazed upon the decrepit figure in astonishment.

"What is the matter with that man?" he asked Chandaka his charioteer.

"There is nothing wrong with him," replied Chandaka, "except that he is old. All men must grow old like that."

A CHINESE WOOD-CUT DRAWING FROM AN EARLY BUDDHIST WORK, DEPICTING BUDDHA AS THE PERSONIFICATION OF WISDOM RISING TRIUMPHANTLY FROM HIS BURIAL CASKET. BUDDHA SEATED IN THE LOTUS CONQUERING DEATH PARALLELS THE CHRISTIAN MYSTICAL RESURRECTION.

——COURTESY OF THE LIBRARY OF CONGRESS.

The prince was profoundly disturbed by what he had seen, and the sages in the upper world nodded their heads gravely. The seed of the Quest had been planted. On another day another vision came. The prince in his riding saw another pitiful figure—a man dying of a horrible disease. Again, he asked his charioteer and Chandaka answered, "That, my Prince, is sickness, and all men are susceptible to it."

"Why does such misery come to mortal beings?" asked the prince.

"We know not why, master," answered the charioteer. "It must be the will of the gods."

Again, the prince thought deeply and again the sages in the heavens smiled. The third vision presented itself under similar conditions. The prince while driving, saw a procession bearing in their midst a corpse. The living were weeping and the dead was cold and grey. "That, master, is death," explained Chandaka, "all men must in the end return to the common clay."

"But what is life?" asked Prince Siddhartha, "if it must all end in this?"

"Man cannot answer such questions," murmured the chariot driver. It was a thoughtful prince who returned to the glitter and youth of his own palace. He had never before known that there was misery. He had never seen anything but youth and beauty and life. He could no longer enjoy his wealth, no longer did his musicians and his poets satisfy him. Then came the last of the visions. The prince beheld a stately figure robed in the simple saffron garment of a monk. There was peace in the face, enlightenment in the eyes. Siddhartha seemed to feel that this monk in his simple garment and rope cord was alone master of life and death.

"That" replied Chandaka in answer to his question, "is a holy man who has renounced the world and lives alone in the mountains, devoting his life to good works and meditation."

When Prince Siddhartha returned to his palace, he had already determined in his mind the course he would pursue. The urge within him, the urge of ages, called him to the monastic life. The Reincarnated Sage was beginning to remember, longing again for the life of wisdom. King Suddhodana had observed the gloomy, melancholy turn that had come to his son. Fearfully, he ordered all of the gates to be guarded so that his son might not escape into the world of sorrow. But the Arhats in the Tushita heaven willed otherwise. The guards slumbered, for a sleep had descended upon them from the heavens and they could not resist. Softly, the young prince roused himself. For a moment, he stood over the couch of his wife and infant son. He picked his way carefully among the scattered forms of sleeping revelers. Chandaka met him at the palace door. Swiftly, the chariot sped through the night. There was no sound for the Lokapalas, beings of the invisible world, held up the horses' hoofs. They passed without challenge through the gates that opened by magic as they approached. The sleeping guards were not aroused and the prince with his faithful charioteer rode on into the night.

When they were safely away from the palace, Prince Siddhartha stopped the chariot, and removing his jewels, gave them to Chandaka. Then with a knife, he cut off his princely lock of hair, tossing it to the winds where the hairs were picked up by little spirits and taken away. He then changed his soft garments for a rough hunter's garb, and after affectionately parting from his faithful friend, walked slowly down the dusty road, without money and without food, carrying in his hand the beggar's bowl.

Gautama Siddhartha was entirely sincere in his quest for truth. He searched in the only place that he knew that is in the communities of recluses and among the hermits that lived in caves in the rocky sides of mountains. He learned something from them all, but not one could give him the answers to the three questions which he always propounded. Meeting a holy man, Siddhartha would greet him and say, "Tell me, venerable sir, where did we come from? why are we here? and where do we go?" Always there was silence. Then there was talking about other things, but never a solution to these fundamental questions.

A pilgrim as devout as the young prince could scarcely fail to have disciples. Other mendicants, observing his zeal in spiritual matters, attached themselves to him, and, as a little group wandered up and down the countryside. This was also the period of fasting, for in India, all holy men fast. Less and less, the prince ate in the hope that the weakening of his body might bring with it the enlightenment of his inner self. But even fasting was in vain. He was finally no longer able to walk. Disciples less devout than himself helped him along. At last, dying of starvation and unable to travel further, Prince Siddhartha was laid gently on the ground by the side of the road to die, his disciples remaining a reverent distance away. Lying by the road, the weakened man summed up his search. Wanderings had gained him nothing, prayers had brought him no solution, fasting had failed, and now he lay dying—the questions unanswered. It was then that the prince decided to eat. He loudly demanded food. His disciples, shocked and amazed, gave him a little of their store and then departed, firmly of the belief that their leader had fallen back into the world of sin.

Strengthened by his food and ended by a villager, the prince slowly regained his health. When he was restored, he resumed his search without any further practice of extreme austerities. There was no one else to go to, no other shrine before which he could pray. Discouraged, weary and broken by six years of constant pilgrimage, he sank to rest on a little knoll under the spreading branches of what is now the sacred banyan tree near Madras. Seated quietly, thus the prince again summed up in his own mind his efforts and tried to understand why he had failed. Suddenly it seemed to him that figures separated themselves from the trees about him and a trooping host of spirits gathered around the little hillock on which he sat. The dancing girls of the palace he had left behind clinked their little cymbals. He could hear the tinkle of anklet bells, and see the whirling figures of the dancers. A voice seemed to speak to him.

"Give it up, it is of no use. Go back to the pleasures you have left behind." "No," replied the prince mentally, "I will never go back. I must discover the answer."

Then among the shadows appeared the figure of his own wife, holding towards him his little son, begging him to return and take up the duties of a father. The old king also held out his arms for his lost son. Still, the prince would not yield. The earth before him opened. Mara, lord of the pit, the prince of evil and his host of demons, sought to tear from him his resolution. But seated quietly under the banyan tree, the prince was unmoved by their demands and their warnings.

At last, the whole vision cleared away and the peace of the night closed in again, with its strange far-off sounds. The mind of the prince went inward. He seemed to be no longer seated under the tree. He felt himself traveling, moving about through all the world, until it seemed that he stood upon every street corner of the earth. He saw men being born, he saw them suffering and dying, and he followed their souls around the mysterious cycle of rebirth until he saw them return again to the earth. The prince seemed to walk within the very hearts of men until he knew their dreaming's, yearnings and longings. His realization ascended into the heavens and mingled with the supernatural beings, even the sages and Arhats that dwelt in the furthermost reaches of the divine worlds.

Then he was back again under the banyan tree. Figures were coming down the sky, sages and saints in their saffron robes and shaven heads. As far as he could see were the circles of monks. They welcomed him, they accepted him into their own order. He was the twenty-ninth Buddha of the divine line.

Then Mara appeared again in the very midst of the circles of the perfected. The tempter speaks, "Go, perfected soul, into the Nirvana. You have earned the rest, the final emancipation." Then voices sounded, voices coming up from somewhere beneath, swelling in upon him from every hand. The faces about him all seemed to speak, in the distance the Lohans were chanting the sacred song: "Teach the Law. Give to men the Way of illumination. Return to earth and spread the doctrine to all the corners of the world that men may dwell in the light of truth."

"I will teach," said the new Buddha. The phantoms faded, and Gautama Buddha, the Light of Asia, sat alone in meditation under the banyan tree. The watches of the night had passed, the shadows were forever dissipated. The liberated man rose and went forth, living the Law and preaching the Law.

The new Buddha had fallen from grace in the eyes of the holy men, for it had been noised about that he had ceased his austerities and had committed the terrible sin of eating like other men. For some time, Buddha had no hearing. It was at Sarnath, outside of Benares, that he was able to preach his first sermon. Advancing along a dusty road, he beheld a little distance ahead of him five of his previous disciples. They were resting on a little hillock by the roadside. Seeing him approach, they said among themselves, "We shall not recognize him or go near him or listen to him, or show any courtesy to him."

Buddha gave little heed to them, but seating himself on a rolling knoll some distance from them, he began preaching. This is the Buddhist Sermon on the Mount, setting forth the principal elements of the philosophy of life. When the discourse was finished the five disciples were at the Master's feet, the first to be accepted into the Doctrine.

After the illumination, Buddha lived to preach for forty-four years. During this time, he travelled through the greater part of India, gathering disciples and implanting his beliefs and teachings in the hearts of thousands. After a few years of preaching, the Buddha marched at the head of a procession of followers. Hundreds of monks in their saffron robes followed him and when he stopped, they gathered about in respectful silence and listened to his words, and of all his disciples the most beloved was Ananda.

Several years after the Illumination, the Buddha, at the request of King Suddhodana, his father, returned to his own city. Here he received his own son Rahula, now a man, and ordained him into the order. At this time, he also accepted Prajapati who was the first woman to be initiated into the order.

When the Buddha was eighty years old, he told Ananda that his life upon the earth was nearly finished and that he only desired to remain long enough to see his work established upon a permanent foundation. During the last years of his life, therefore, he drew his disciples and converts more closely together, laying the foundations of what was afterwards to be his church or institute. His actual death was brought about by the eating of tainted food, given unintentionally by a well-meaning carpenter who was a convert to his order. When the time of the passing of the Master came, the disciples were gathered about in clusters and circles. Ananda was weeping. A couch had been prepared on which the Buddha was resting between the spreading branches of two sola trees. The Buddha turned upon his right side and, rising his head upon his right arm, passed into meditation. From meditation, he moved through one state of consciousness to another until his consciousness achieved the Nirvana. When this had been attained, the body died.

The following day, the remains of the body were cremated. A great funeral pyre was built upon which the body of the Enlightened, still in his saffron robe, was placed with the deepest of veneration. Many efforts were made to light the fire, but they all failed. At last, a flame burst from the heart of the dead Buddha and consumed all. The ashes of the Perfected One were placed in seven urns and conveyed to different parts of Asia, where they were enshrined to perpetuate the memory of Gautama Siddhartha, twenty-ninth Buddha.

THE TEACHINGS OF BUDDHA

The life of Buddha has been ornamented with numerous legends. Every Buddhist country has embellished the story of the Enlightened One and his works. In the same way and from the same motives, the principal elements of the Buddhist philosophy have been variously modified, interpreted and expanded by the peoples and nations that form together the Buddhist world.

In the terms of modern classification, the original Buddhism was a philosophical agnosticism. The first doctrines emphasized codes of conduct and the achievement of enlightenment through the constant practice of certain virtues. As time passed theological elements increased in the cult, until today it assumes all the aspects of a religion, including elaborate ceremonialism, a vast pantheon of divinities and demons, and a priestcraft perpetuated by a process similar to the Apostolic succession of the Roman church. Of course, there are exceptions. All Buddhism has not assumed an ecclesiastical appearance. In Ceylon, the severe philosophical agnosticism of the original sect still survives, but for the most part primitive Buddhism has disappeared and, in its place, has risen the shrines and temples of theologized Buddhism.

Buddhist philosophy was early divided into two distinct schools, called the Hinayana, or small cart, and the Mahayana, or large cart. By cart should be understood "vehicle." The Hinayana was needlessly severe. It offered the advantages of philosophy only to monies and ascetics and held an attitude of Brahmanical aloofness towards that very multitude which Buddha himself sought to instruct. While the Hinayana escaped the elaborate ecclesiasticism of the "great cart" it also lost the gentle universality of the original revelation. It is natural that a severe, exacting, uncompromising and dictatorial sect would not become very popular, especially to the peasant mind, Mahayana met this need. It offered the salvation of the Buddhist doctrines to men of every class and hind. The great and the lowly travelled the same road. By virtuous conduct, all in the end attained the common good. Thus, it appears that the Mahayana school was originally closer to the beliefs of Buddha. On the other hand, its very democracy and simplicity led inevitably to a multitude of misunderstandings. High places in the order were occupied by men essentially sincere but hopelessly uninformed. Gradually the principles of the doctrine were warped by misunderstanding, idolatry crept in, ritual gained an over-significance. At last magic and sorcery with its incantations and propitiations of demons, its traffic in relics and charms, and most of all its relaxing emphasis upon the philosophy of life, diverted the Mahayana sect from the nobility of its original purpose. Many brilliant reformers sought to restore the purity of Buddha's doctrine, but unfortunately the reforms became cults in themselves, until a general confusion obscured the entire subject.

A few small groups have preserved the integrity of the original teaching and it is to these groups that the modern seeder must turn in order to secure a proper perspective on the subject of Buddhist philosophy. The collapse of modern civilization must bring with it a restatement of religious and philosophic purposes. The non-Buddhist world is beginning to recognize the scope and profundity of Buddha's doctrine. A world sorely in need of a workable philosophy is turning towards the East and is being richly rewarded for its effort.

Buddhism combines the elements of profundity and simplicity. So profound that only the wisest of men can hope to fully comprehend it, so simple that a child can grasp its purposes, the Buddhist philosophy is capable of serving simultaneously both the depth and the shallowness in mankind. The doctrine is founded upon moral precepts and from this simple beginning; it ascends gradually to the most abstract of metaphysical speculations. A monk entering the order is bound by a very severe code of proprieties, which are termed the Ten Commandments of Buddhism. He vows:

To kill no living thing.

To accept nothing that is not given willingly.

To live in absolute moral purity.

To speak only the truth.

To touch no animal food or alcohol.

To eat only at prescribed times.

To abstain from all unnecessary contacts with the world.

To wear no ornament.

To avoid all luxury.

To live always in voluntary poverty.

In Protestant Buddhist countries, such as Japan, these regulations are modified even by the priesthood, much as in the case of the Protestant Reformation in Europe. But even in a modified form, the Buddhist code is one of the most strict in the world, and more amazing still to the Western mind, is the absolute fidelity with which it is lived. Dishonesty and intemperance are seldom met with among Buddhist peoples. They not only accept their doctrines, they live them.

The Noble Eight-fold Path is for both the clergy and the laity, and next to the Practice of the

Virtues is the most important of the Buddhist disciplines. The living of the Eight Truths infers a constant and consistent doing of the following things:

1. The holding of Right Attitude, at all times free from prejudice, illusion, superstition, doubts, fears and animosities.

2. The living of the highest standard of conduct which the mind can conceive; living the truth one knows.

3. The control of speech so that it is always true, simple, gentle and entirely honest.

4. Right conduct. Honest, just and enlightened relationship with other living things.

5. The practice of harmlessness. To live without hurting, either by killing or injuring physically, or the causing of sorrow, mental or emotional.

6. Perseverance in noble action. The overcoming of all of the elements of the illusional life.

7. Right thinking. The directing of the mind towards the understanding of the supreme wisdom.

8. Right meditation. The practice of the Inner Experience.

To accomplish the Eight-fold Path, it is necessary to overcome ten "fetters" or forms of bondage. These are called Illusions and are listed as follows:

1. The illusion that the soul is immortal.

2. The illusion that there is no way of accomplishing salvation.

3. The illusion that external religious rites, prayers, sermons, sacrifices and other ceremonies will lead to salvation.

4. The illusion of the senses and passions.

5. The illusion of hatred and malevolence.

6. The illusion of the love of this life and of the world.

7. The illusion of a future life, whether in heaven or paradise.

8. The illusion of pride.

9. The illusion of superciliousness.

10. The illusion of ignorance.

It should be evident from the preceding how strict a standard of living and thinking the Buddhist must live up to, yet these words which seem to place so many boundaries upon human life and thought have not the inhibiting, narrowing sense that the ignorant mind supposes. They all rise from realization, the accomplishment of the right attitude. When a man has the right attitude, he instinctively practices the virtues for no other course of procedure is acceptable. It is impossible for a man to truly believe one thing and do another. To love truth is to practice truth, to love wisdom is to live consistently with wisdom. The path of Buddha is the living of the Law, the Law being in this sense the standard of right, living in a manner consistent with the nobility of a human creature. All that is not noble is unworthy of man and man should never be less than himself.

To summarize briefly the Buddhist concept of life and the reason for the disciplines imposed upon the disciple: The universe is composed of different qualities, or possibly more accurately, conditions of consciousness. The whole of nature is composed of different modes of realization or the inward knowledge of truth. The gods, so-called, are highly evolved forms of consciousness, not entities or beings, but rather degrees of truth. The universe throughout all its parts is filled with a mysterious essence called Self, much as the Christians teach that the universe is filled with Spirit.

This universal all-pervading Self is the Reality in all natures, and the perfection of every so-called created thing is achieved by its reabsorption into this Universal Self. This reabsorption, the Buddhist symbolizes by a drop of water falling into the sea. The drop of water in this case represents an individual, and the sea Universal Self. By this concept, there is nothing immortal in man, for instead of the spirit he has at the root of himself, only Universal Self. Personality is illusion, universality is the only truth.

The purpose of life is to wear out or overcome the illusions which result in separate existences. This does not mean that illusions are non-existent, but rather impermanent. The Buddhist does not say that material phenomenon is an optical illusion. He acknowledges the existence of what he sees, but not the reality of it, reality in the sense of importance or significance. Thus, there are many men but only one Self, there are trees, flowers, birds and animals but only one Self. There are suns, moons and stars, but only one Self. Self in the greatest, and the Self in the least are one and identical.

The absolute universality of the individual is called Nirvana or the end of illusion. The Buddhist calls the phenomenal universe the Not-Self. The grass grows and dies; man is born and in time disappears again; even the suns must sometime fall from the heavens. All that is Not-Self must finally cease and vanish away. Only the Self remains, eternal and unconditioned. It requires many millions of years to hill out illusion in the heart of man. It is quite impossible for him to accomplish this in a single life. Therefore, Buddhism explains the mystery of the inequalities and inconsistencies of life by means of two inflexible and immutable Laws—Reincarnation and Karma—to which there cannot at any time, under any condition, ever be an exception.

Reincarnation teaches that man returns to this world life after life, dedicated ultimately to the one purpose of hilling out the illusion within himself. In each life, man performs various actions, arising from his belief in illusion. Some men steal, others hill, and others seek to horde up treasures. These actions because they are inconsistent with absolute truth, result in Karma or consequence, for as Buddha said: "Effect follows cause as the wheel of the cart follows the foot of the oxen." The evils we do in one life return to us as misfortune in the next. So, we continue, incarnation after incarnation, until the doing of evil dies out within us and wisdom takes the place of ignorance.

The heavens and hells of Buddhism are the conditions of consciousness in which men live. A man whose heart is filled with hate must abide in an inferno of his own making. Wisdom brings with it peace and peace is paradise. Men do not go to heaven or hell when they die. They live it throughout their lives according to the measure of their own understanding, their own good and evil impulses.

The principal purpose of the Buddhist organization is to perpetuate the simple truth that suffering is the result of wrong action, and happiness and security are the rewards of right thinking and virtuous living. Wars cause wars, evil perpetuates evil, but all evil ceases when truth is revealed and is enthroned victoriously in the heart of men.

The Middle Path of Buddhism ends finally in the accomplishment of Nirvana. The truth seeker becomes one with Truth, the dreamer becomes identical with his dream. Man does not become wise, he becomes wisdom; he is merged into the very essence of the virtue which he has accomplished. Thus, it is that a perfected man is the Buddha—not a Buddha but the buddha. Buddha means enlightenment. He who receives enlightenment is the Buddha, for there is only one Truth and when all men reach that truth, then all men are one. Not of one mind only but of one substance and one essence, and in the end the truth seeker is absorbed into that very Reality which sustains the whole far-flung panorama of life and death, ignorance and wisdom, beginning and end.

QUOTATIONS FROM THE DHAMMAPADA
AND OTHER EARLY BUDDHIST WRITINGS
ATTRIBUTED TO BUDDHA

"They blame him who sits silent, they blame him who speaks much, they also blame him who says little, there is no one on earth who is not blamed."

"A man is not learned because he talks much; he who is patient, free from hatred and pain, he is called learned."

"As a solid rock is not shaken by the wind, wise people falter not amidst blame and praise."

"He who, seeking his own happiness, injures or destroys other beings who also long for happiness, will not find happiness even after death."

"The fool finally becomes full of evil even though he gathers it little by little."

"Earnestness is the path of immortality, thoughtlessness the path of death; those who are in earnest do not die, those who are thoughtless are as if dead already."

"If one man conquers in battle a thousand times a thousand men, and if another conquers himself, this last is the greater of the conquerors."

"As a bee collects nectar, and departs without injuring the flower, or its color or scent, so let a sage dwell in his village."

Yours sincerely,

Manly P. Hall

AUGUST 15, 1936

Dear Friend,

ZOROASTER

Zarathustrism, or Zoroastrianism as it is more commonly called, was the ancient faith of the Irano-Aryan peoples who at some remote period migrated from India and civilized Persia, Media and other parts of ancient Chaldea. According to the earliest tradition, the Magian Rites of the Persians were established by the fire-prophet Zarathustra, but no reliable information is available as to the exact time of his life and ministry. He is variously placed from the first to the tenth millennium before Christ. This uncertainty results in part at least from the destruction of the libraries of the Magian philosophers by the armies of Alexander the Great.

Zarathustra, in Greek Zoroaster, is a generic name bestowed upon several initiated and divinely illumined law-givers and religious reformers among the Chaldeans. As in the case of Manu and Vyasa in India, Moses in Israel, Orpheus in Greece and Quetzalcoatl in Mexico, time has corrupted into one personality several Magian philosophers by the name of Zarathustra. The result has been a pseudo-historical account in which the actions of several men are fitted together to make one highly metaphysical tradition. The different parts can probably never be properly ordered because the Zend language is utterly extinct and the old records have found no perpetuators in the modern world.

Greek's writers derive the term Zoroaster from a combination of syllables so that the word can have one of several meanings. First, a worshipper of the stars. Second, the image of secret things. Third, a fashioner of images from hidden fire. Or most probably, fourth, the son of the stars.

The oldest of the Iranian books, called the Sesatir, contains a collection of teachings and revelations from fourteen of the ancient prophets of Iran, and in this list, Zoroaster stands thirteenth. It is not improbable that at some prehistoric time a great sage, an initiate of the original Mysteries of the Aryan Hindus, established the line of priest-prophets which came later to bear his name and finally became identified with him. There is ample precedent for such a circumstance, for in the Hermetic tradition of the Egyptians many generations of initiate priests lost their identity and were absorbed into the one all-powerful word, Hermes. Greek writers distinguish at least six Zoroaster's. The first was a Chaldean, the second a Bactrian, the third a Persian, the fourth a Pamphylia, the fifth Proconnesian, and the sixth a Babylonian. The last of these, according to Apuleius, was a contemporary of Pythagoras who visited and studied with him when Pythagoras was carried a prisoner to Babylon by the armies of Cambyses.

Space prevents a detailed examination of the conflicting accounts relative to the comparative importance of these several Zoroasters and it is questionable whether even an exhaustive analysis of the information available would result in any conclusions of primary importance. The student should rather bear in mind that Zoroaster as he descends to us in modern history is the personification of a noble philosophical system founded by a semi-divine mortal at a remote period in the world's history, and carried on by a line of consecrated priests until its final dissipation by the Mohammedans.

With these restrictions, we can summarize briefly the more or less legendary story of Zarathustra's life. For reasons which should be apparent from the foregoing, it is not even possible to describe with anything approaching accuracy the appearance or the temperament of the founder of the Magian Rites. The portrait of Zarathustra which accompanies this article is believed to be the only existing likeness of the old prophet. The original is a rock carving of unknown age the face of which was mutilated beyond recognition and reconstructed by some pious believer whose faith probably greatly exceeded his array of facts. Although this portrait is generally accepted as a likeness of the Magus, there is every possible doubt as to its authenticity. Those best qualified to pass an opinion on the subject hazard the guess that the sculpture was intended to represent Ahura-Mazda, the First Principle of the world in the Persian belief. The face may have been destroyed by some zealous Zoroastrian for the members of this faith are strongly opposed to idolatry. On the other hand, it may have been mutilated by the Greeks or Mohammedans. From a metaphysical viewpoint, it is by no means impossible that the carving represented Ahura-Mazda personified in the form of Zoroaster, his beloved prophet.

Even modern authorities are not in agreement as to the date of Zoroaster's ministry. The present tendency however is to narrow down the time to the period between 1200 and 500 B.C. That a great prophet did arise in Iran during these centuries has been established as a historical certainty, but that other prophets preceded him in the propounding of the Magian philosophy is generally acknowledged as a possibility. Modern scholars view the Greek and Roman traditions rather dubiously. The Buddhist tradition in India emphatically affirms that Gautama Siddhartha was not the first

Buddha, but rather the principal exponent of the Buddhist system. We have the same problem in Persia. While the sacred scriptures make mention of several ancient prophets, Zarathustra Spitama is acknowledged as the chief exponent of the Magian doctrines.

A. V. Williams Jackson, in his important book ZOROASTER THE PROPHET OF ANCIENT IRAN, published by the Columbia University Press, examines critically yet impartially the available data relative to the life and time of Zoroaster and advances a well-supported opinion that Zarathustra Spitama was born on the first day of the year B.C. 660 and died on the forty-first day of the year B.C. 583, being then at the age of seventy-seven years and forty-one days. This is the time generally agreed upon by Par see scholars, but other European authors advance a somewhat earlier date.

According to the Gathas the Prophet was born at Azerbaijan in Western Iran. As in the case of Jesus, an effort is made to trace his ancestry back to the princes of his land. It is recorded that his father's name was Pourushaspa and his mother's Dughdhova. He was the third of five sons. Most accounts agree that Zoroaster was born of an Immaculate Conception. The legend tells that his father, in performing religious ceremonials, drank the sacred homa juice which is the same as the soma of the Hindus, the mysterious drink of the gods. As a result, his wife conceived without knowing a man. The nativity was accompanied by supernatural manifestations and occult circumstances appropriate to the incarnation of an Avatar or divine being. It is said that all nature rejoiced at the birth of the Prophet. Ahriman, the genius of evil, and his host of demons, all hid themselves in the darkest parts of the earth to escape the splendor of the newborn sage. At the time of the incarnation, a ring of heavenly light surrounded the house of Pourushaspa. According to a most ancient Greek's tradition, Zoroaster is the only mortal ever to laugh at the moment of birth. It is also said that while he was an infant, his brain throbbed so that it violently pushed away a hand as if it was placed upon his head. The Greeks also have a somewhat different tradition which says that Zoroaster was the son of Oromasdes the spirit of fire, but the word Oromasdes seems to be a Grecianized form of Ahura-Mazda, the spirit of eternal light, the first active Principle in the Zoroastrian cosmogony.

The demons being unable to prevent the birth of the Prophet, immediately seek his destruction. Many efforts were made to slay him while still a babe, but through miraculous intercession, he escaped his enemies. The Turanian Karap, Durasrobo, played the part of Herod in the Zoroastrian story. He was a worshipper of idolatrous gods and was served by a priestcraft of sorcerers. The Karap and his religious advisers, though unable to destroy the child, so influenced Pourushaspa that he turned from his own son, fearing him to be a demon born in human form. But the infant discomfited his adversaries and we next hear of him at his seventh year, a precocious and amazing child who is given into the peeping of a wise and venerable sage to be educated in the mysteries of the true religion. At about this time he also escapes an effort to poison him, for the hosts of Ahriman were determined that the Prophet should never preach in Iran.

It was the custom of that time for a boy to reach his majority at the age of fifteen and it is expressly stated that at this age he was initiated into the true faith, a ceremony which always took place at the time of the majority. At this time also his father, now reconciled with his divine son, divided his properties among his children. Zoroaster chose only a mysterious belt for his share of the patrimony. At this time also the young man was invested with the Kusti or sacred thread or cord, the symbol of the ancient Mazdean faith. Already the young man was turning toward a religious life and at twenty he assumed religious orders and left home. He went out alone to fast and meditate in the Persian desert. Practically his only food during that time was a certain sacred cheese which never grew old or moldy.

There may be a connection between this account and the mysterious food of Hercules which Pythagoras ate while similarly fasting in desert places. At one time during his life, Zoroaster was supposed to have lived in a sacred mountain in a deep cavern. The area where he dwelt was surrounded day and night by a ring of flames. The Prophet could pass through this sacred fire without danger, but unbelievers attempting to follow him were immediately consumed.

At thirty, Zoroaster began his ministry. With a small group of followers, he traveled into Iran and on at least one occasion performed a miracle similar to that attributed to Moses, for he caused a sea to part and with his followers passed through the waters on dry land. It was on May 5th precisely at dawn that Zoroaster received his first vision. He was by the side of a river. Suddenly there appeared before him the vast figure of Vohumano. The celestial being told him to cast aside his body and follow him. He was lifted up into the presence of Ahura-Mazda. Here he received from the lips of the Eternal Power the doctrines he was to teach. After this first vision, there came six others dealing principally with the secrets of the angels. He beheld the Amesha-Spentas, the angelic and archangelic hosts. The visions being completed, the Prophet, initiated in divine mysteries, then faced the temptation. Ahriman and the hosts of the inferno tried in every way to destroy the Prophet or turn him from his course. The temptation of Zoroaster follows in general the temptation of Buddha under the bodhi tree, or that of Jesus on the side of Tabor. Victorious over all of the forces of evil, and armed with righteousness, Zoroaster discomfited Ahriman and scattered his evil spirits.

The Prophet's first convert was his own cousin, then, following the orders of Ahura-Mazda, Zoroaster spent the eleventh and twelfth years of his mission (which began at thirty) in the conversion of the powerful Prince Vishtaspa. He was to become the Constantine of Zoroastrianism, like Asoka of Buddhism. The conversion of Vishtaspa was the most important episode in the life of the Prophet. This powerful Iranian prince, surrounded by his court, ministers and priests, was seated upon his throne in the royal palace at Balkh. Suddenly the great stones that formed the roof of the palace slowly opened as though by magic and through the entrance thus formed the Prophet descended in the air bearing a cube of fire in one hand and a scepter of cypress wood in the other. Zoroaster seems to have been a powerfully built man who wore white robes and a turban-like cap with a long streamer. Thus attired, he faced King Vishtaspa. According to the law of the day he was examined by the priests and philosophers and after three days of constant questioning, Zoroaster was victorious.

The priests of the perverted state faith, jealous and fearful of his power, caused a number of objects used in sorcery to be concealed in his house. He was then arrested as a sorcerer and thrown into prison, but Ahura-Mazda reached the king in his weakest spot. Vishtaspa was a great horseman and prided himself upon the spirit of his horses. When Zoroaster was arrested the king's favorite black horse was instantly paralyzed. Vishtaspa sensed this circumstance as a divine warning and released the Prophet. At this time also he was converted to the faith. The black horse immediately and miraculously recovered. The conversion of Vishtaspa was followed by the conversion of most of his court. The new religion became the official faith of the country. Zoroaster had accomplished his mission and the idolatrous cults were gradually abolished in the land. Then followed years of wandering up and down through Iran. There is a tradition that Zoroaster visited Egypt, also India and Greece. But these traditions stand on their own merits. There is no way of proving them at this distant time. It is recorded of the Prophet that he performed miracles including the curing of blindness.

The deadly enemy of Vishtaspa was the Turonian prince Arejat-aspa the warlike Turk. He invaded Vishtaspa's kingdom. Isfandiar, the son of Vishtaspa, and a convert to the Zoroastrian faith, led the armies of Iran and defeated Arejat-aspa. Returning home victoriously, Isfandiar expected to receive the crown from his father's hands. But a younger brother had calumniated him before the king and Isfandiar was thrown into prison as a reward for his courage and devotion.

Some years passed and again Arejat-aspa invaded the lands of Iran. Vishtaspa was away from his kingdom. Isfendiar was in prison. The armies of Iran were defeated. Arejat-aspa captured Balkh and destroyed the Zoroastrian temple of Mush-Adar. He pillaged the Zoroastrian shrine, extinguished the sacred fire, slew the priests, and killed Zoroaster.

The description of the death of the Magian as told by the Persians is to the effect that he was performing the sacred offices of the temple when the Turanian invaders burst in. One of the barbarians threw his spear at the Prophet while he knew in prayer before the altar. Zoroaster, mortally wounded, turned and threw his rosary at the assassin who fell as though struck by a bolt of lightning. Vishtaspa, learning of the tragedy, releases Isfendier who leads an army against Arejat-aspa. The armies of the Turanian are finally defeated and Arejat-aspa himself put to the sword.

The Greek account of the death of the Prophet is to the effect that a great flame descended from the constellation of Orion and gathered up his immortal remains. This sheet of celestial fire which consumed him was the fiery body of his father who gathered up his illustrious son and bore him back to the starry heavens from which he had come.

According to Suidas, Zoroaster left four books of which one is concerned with the mystery of astrology, the others with moral and political matters. Among the mystics of Persia, there is still currently a legend describing a certain great cavern near the summit of a high peak of the Thian-Shan mountains where are preserved to this day tablets of the original Zarathustra. In some future date, these tablets shall be rescued from oblivion when the world has grown wise enough to interpret the secret mysteries inscribed thereon.

THE ZOROASTRIAN DOCTRINE

The Avesta is the principal religious book of the Zoroastrians. The Avesta, with its Zend or interpretation, is usually erroneously called the Zend-Avesta. The Gathas of the Avesta record the actual words of the prophet. Other parts of the book contain doctrines attributed to him, and commentary material. The Avesta is still the principal text of the Parsee communities in India. Existing versions of the Avesta are of comparatively late composition. The earliest date from the 12th century of the Christian era. There is considerable difference in existing manuscripts of the Avesta, indicating they were derived from more extensive originals or a considerable body of tradition from which various selections were made. The Avesta, as it stands today, is the last of an imposing literature, the greater part of which is now lost to the world. Tradition tells that the Avesta was originally compiled by Zoroaster, written upon twelve thousand hides which were bound together with golden bands. The writing was in the secret and sacred language of the prophet of which it is the only example. The characters were supposedly given to Zoroaster by the angels.

Although Zoroaster was unquestionably one of the greatest original thinkers of antiquity, it should not be supposed that he evolved his entire theology without contact with other religious systems. The roots of Zoroastrianism are deep in the primitive folk-lore of the Irano-Aryan peoples. Brahmanism, Chaldean philosophy, Egyptian metaphysics, and even Chinese traditions appear as elements in the Magian doctrine. Zoroaster's contribution was a new interpretation of the older beliefs. The nobility of his intellect is best revealed in his appreciation of spiritual values at a time when most men were bound by narrow and literal codes.

The ancient Zoroastrian doctrines were an extraordinary compound of monotheism, anthropomorphism and pantheism. The beginning of Persian philosophy is the establishment of the nature of the First Principle of existence, hike the Chaldeans and Egyptians, the Zoroastrians define First Cause as an infinite extension, an absolute diffusion of life. Activity they symbolize by a line extending infinitely in union with itself—a circle. The Persians regard the circle in the same way that the Greeks and Egyptians do—the absolute pattern of divine activity. Behind all the Persian philosophy, there is an absolute extension of being—the Space God—the boundless circle of unknown Time. This unknown, unaging and unpassing Principle they term Zeroana Akerne.

Out of Zeroana A kerne emerges the radiant, glorious, manifested creator—Ahura-Mazda—space objectified as a gigantic entity. Zeroana Akerne, the Thrice-Deep Darkness, contains ever within itself the power of objectification. Periodically AhuraMazda, the Logos, comes forth, manifests for a certain time, then retires again into the Eternal Darkness. Space, Zeroana Akerne, has two aspects—unmanifesting and manifesting. When Space manifests it is Ahura-Mazda; when it is unmanifested, it is Zeroana Akerne.

Ahura-Mazda is a triad, a blazing triangle established in the darkness of Eternal Life. Ahura is the eternal wisdom; Mazda is the vehicle of that wisdom; and Ahura-Mazda together is the light of knowledge manifesting before the created world. It appears that in some of the earlier works Zoroaster is regarded as the incarnation of Ahura-Mazda, at least his manifestor before men. Therefore, it is said that Zoroaster had three sons, a king, a warrior and a priest, these representing the triad of powers which manifest from the light of God.

Light manifesting in darkness creates contrast or combat, and from this contrast comes the principle of evil, the darkness always seeking to swallow up the light. The luminous being, Ahura-Mazda, moving in the midst of space, formed the universe and incarnated himself in the luminous parts of the world, finally manifesting as Ormuzd the sun. The sun, as materially objectified light, battles with the darkness to sustain the life of the world. Spirit and matter are thus contrasted. By the union of spirit and matter, forms are created and, in each form, there is a conflict, and this conflict in men is called the struggle between the higher and lower Self. The lower or grosser elements are always regarded as the Adversary or the impediment. This Adversary is termed Ahriman, the serpent. When Ahura-Mazda, as the creative intellect, began the fabrication of living things, Ahriman, the negator, created shadows or bodies in which the luminous principles were imprisoned. Thus, we have a new triad consisting of Ahura-Mazda, Ormuzd and Ahriman; or spirit, soul and body, the creating, preserving and destroying phases of existence—the Brahma, Vishnu and Shiva of the Hindus.

The old Persians were astro-philosophers. They used astrology as a symbolical science to represent the mystery of creation, using the zodiac as a key. They said that during the first three signs, the gods were created. Aries was Zeroana Akerne, Taurus was Ahura-Mazda, and Gemini the twins was the third Logos, the duality Ormuzd-Ahriman. AhuraMazda then caused to issue out of his own nature six secondary divinities which, with himself, constituted the septenary. These are called the Amesha-Spentas, the seven gods of the dawn, the Cosmocratores, the World Builders, the Elohim, or the Dhyana Buddhas. The seven gods created the seven worlds. They are the spectrum, the seven tones, and finally descending through different states of consciousness, become the seven planets of the ancient solar system. They build the seven heavens and the seven earths. Ahura-Mazda incarnates himself in the first heaven, the sphere of Saturn, and sends forth his six regents. He then incarnates again in the lowest world and sending out his six manifestations creates continents. Thus, the seven are the divine keepers of the earth—the Lords of the divisions of time and place. They are the seven patriarchs, and the seven stars of the Little Bear, the mysterious constellation within which moves the mysterious axis of the pole.

When Ahura-Mazda sends forth the six divinities out of himself, a similar phenomenon manifests in the shadow world below. Six demons emerge from Ahriman to become the adversaries of the gods. These are the spirits of evil, and from them, issue the seven vices to oppose the seven cardinal virtues.

According to Persian tradition, the world lasts for 12,000 years, but by these years we are to understand twelve great periods of time. These periods are divided into two parts, each of 6000 years, and each of these in turn are divided into two parts of 2000 years, the whole being the great circle of the Zodiac. The Persians break the Zodiac into a quaternary of three signs each, and into an upper and lower hemisphere of six signs each. Ahura-Mazda creates twelve izeds, principles of light. These twelve are the equatorial constellations. At the same time, he created other constellations which are nonzodiacal. The two hosts of gods that fight on the great battlefield of space are the stars of the Northern and Southern hemispheres, the Suras and Asuras of the Hindus. Aries to Libra are the six Lords that issued from the radiant principle of Ahura-Mazda, and Virgo to Pisces are the rebellious angels who, created in the light, became the servants of Ahriman. In the sign of Libra, we have the head of the Great Serpent, and most of the constellation of the Hydra at the beginning of the dark half of the Zodiac is Libra and in it is the head of the serpent of evil. Libra, therefore is the sign of Ahriman, the anti-Christ, the Adversary, the Fallen Man.

In the first 3000 years, that is three signs' Aries, Taurus and Gemini, Ahura-Mazda dwells in the light of his own presence. This is the age of the gods. In the second 3000 years, the creation of the universe takes place. Out of

Cancer, the Great Mother, the Avatar principle of the world is formed. At the point between Virgo and Libra, man is created, the progeny of the celestial Virgin. Thus, the six days of creation. Then the kingdom of Ahriman is established. He controls the world for three cycles—Libra, Scorpio and Sagittarius. In the last 3000 years, the progeny of the divine instructor, the Centaur, break the rule of Ahriman. The battle of Armageddon takes place. Ahriman is defeated by Ormuzd and through his repentance is restored to the light. Therefore, at the end of nine cycles, the divine age is restored. In the last 3000 years, or cycle, the universal kingdom is returned to Ahura-Mazda and his son Sarosh, the Messiah. At the end of 12000 years, or twelve cycles, comes the Deluge which is Pisces. The universe is absorbed back into its original Cause. Ahura-Mazda draws all things back into the Primitive Nature and returns to sleep, where, like the Vishnu of the Hindus, he floats upon the waters of the Abyss, the couch of the seven serpents—the Amesha-Spentas.

From this, we get a new triad of principles:

1. Ahura-Mazda the manifested Logos, the First Principle of the creating triad. Out of him issues:

2. Sarosh the Messiah, the second Logos, the Word. This being is the breath of the Creator, the mouth born son.

3. Zarathustra, upon whom the Word descends, the Perfect Prophet, the word made flesh.

The seven Amesha-Spentas become incarnate in man, his seven bodies, his seven principles, his seven vital organs. These are the creators manifesting their energies in the sustaining of the body. The perfection of man is the Great Work. The good and evil cease when Truth is established. Wisdom destroys all the shadows in which lurk the evil genius of Ahriman. Darkness is not destroyed by violence but is dissipated by the very presence of light. The moment man contains within himself the source of light, the illusions of Ahriman disappear. Wisdom is the mysterious fire within, symbolized by the flame on the Zoroastrian altar. As fire consumes the wood, so the flame of truth consumes the lower elements created by Ahriman.

QUOTATIONS

"Commit no slander; so that infamy and wickedness may not happen unto thee. For it is said that slander is more grievous than witchcraft."

"Form no covetous desire, so that the demon of greediness may not deceive thee, and the treasure of the world may not be tasteless to thee."

"Suffer no anxiety, for he who is a sufferer of anxiety becomes regardless of enjoyment of the world and the spirit, and contraction happens to his body and soul."

"May the Creator of Wisdom teach me his ordinances through Good Thought, that my tongue may have a pathway."

"Thou shouldst not become presumptuous through much treasure and wealth; for in the end, it is necessary for thee to leave all."

"Turn yourself, not away from three best things—GOOD THOUGHT, GOOD WORD, and GOOD DEED."

"Purity is for man, next to life, the greatest good."

"The law of Mazda cleanses the faithful from every evil thought, word and deed, as a swift-rushing, mighty wind cleanses the plain."

"With enemies fight with equity. With a friend proceed with the approval of friends. With a malicious man carry on no conflict, and do not molest him in any way whatever. With a greedy man thou shouldst not be a partner, and do not trust him with the leadership. With an ill-famed man form no connection. With an ignorant man thou shouldst not become a confederate and associate. With a foolish man make no dispute. With a drunken man do not walk on the road. From an ill-natured man take no loan."

"Think purely, speak purely and act purely" is the sum and substance of the ever-diving law which Zoroaster preached to the world.

Sincerely yours,

Manly P. Hall

SEATTLE, WASH., SEPTEMBER 15, 1936

Dear Friend,

PLATO, THE DIVINE MAN

Plato, one of the noblest men who ever lived upon this earth, was born on the day of the Feast of Apollo on the island of Ægina, of an illustrious family. There is some confusion as to the exact date. According to one account, he was born on the 26th or 27th of May, B.C. 427, and according to another, the 5th or 6th of June B.C. 428. He died at Athens B.C. 347, and the earlier date of his birth is most probably correct, for it is explicitly stated that he died in his 81st year.

Apuleius reports that Plato was born of a "sublime race," possibly concurring with Aristander who, with a number of the earlier Platonists, believed the great philosopher to be the son of no mortal man but of the Holy Spirit which manifested itself in the luminous shape of Apollo. Clearchus, in his eulogy of Plato, and Anaxyelids, in his second book of philosophers, Plutarch, Suidas, and others affirm it to have been commonly reported at Athens that Plato was the son of Apollo who appeared in a vision to Perictione, Plato's mother. Plato's father, or foster-father, Aristo, named the babe Aristocles after the paternal grandfather, but as the child grew up, he so increased in size that the name of Plato was conferred upon him in allusion to the largeness of his person, some say the width of his shoulders. Neathes relates the term to the breadth of his forehead, Plato meaning breadth as in the word plateau.

According to Hesychius, Plato was also called Serapis from the majesty and dignity of his person. The gods bestowed upon Plato most of the blessings which can be derived from nature. It was said of him that there was not any imperfection throughout his person. He had "large eloquence," comeliness of body and majesty of intellect. He was a lover of the fine arts, as he learned to paint and addicted himself to poetry. The beauty of his words caused it to be reported of him that while as a child he lay sleeping the bees made a honeycomb in his mouth. In writing he was fluent, in discourse and argument he demonstrated the greatest ability, and in all forms of learning he possessed what the Greeks called an "intensive genius." Stanley, in his history of philosophy, says of Plato that "he added much to learning and languages by many inventions, as well of things as of words." He excelled in grammar and rhetoric, creating many terms now used in these sciences. He had strength of body, love of argument and courage of conviction. He was most proficient in wrestling and even competed in the Pythian games, distinguishing himself in contests of skill and strength. He defended his ideas with great brilliancy and in discourse and debate fearlessly pressed his opinions to their legitimate ends.

Plato became a disciple of Socrates when he was twenty years of age and remained with him for about eight years. At the trial of Socrates, Plato attempted to defend his master but was cried down by the Senate. He later offered to secure the necessary funds to purchase the liberty of Socrates but this the old Athenian sage would not permit. After the death of his master, Plato fled to Megara to escape the animosity of those Athenians who had brought about the death of Socrates and were bent upon the destruction of his school.

The night before Plato presented himself to Socrates as a disciple, Socrates dreamed that a young swan had flown from Cupid's altar in the Academy and had settled to rest in his lap, and after remaining for a short time had taken wing again and flown upward to the heavens where it was received with the greatest delight by the gods and heroes. When Aristo came to Athens and presented his son Plato, Socrates turned to his followers exclaiming "Friends, this is the swan from Cupid's altar!"

Plato was not fully satisfied with the knowledge which he secured from Socrates and determined to perfect himself in a diviner form of wisdom. To achieve this end, he attached himself to Cratylus, a follower of the sect of Heraclitus, into which sect he seems to have been initiated, later he studied with Hermogenes. Having dedicated his life to the discovery of truth, Plato was resolved to travel into any country where wisdom might be found, even if it be to the furthermost parts of the earth, therefore it was natural that he should go to Italy where he could attach himself to the disciplines of the Pythagoreans. There is evidence that, from the Pythagoreans, Plato gained much of natural and divine philosophy. Having discovered that the Pythagoreans in turn had gained much from other nations, he next traveled to Cyrene, where he studied geometry with Theodorus. Next, he went to Egypt to study astrology from the priests there, for, says Cicero, "he learned from the barbarians (Egyptians) arithmetic and celestial speculations." Having surveyed the whole of Egypt, he settled finally in the province of Sais where he studied with the wise men concerning the origin of the universe, the immortality of the soul, and the transmigrations of the soul through earthly bodies. Having accomplished this, he returned to his own nation, regretting that the Eastern wars had prevented his journeying to India.

It may therefore be said of the Platonic philosophy that it is derived from several ancient and mysterious origins. In addition to the illumination which proceeded from his own soul, Plato received knowledge from the Hermetic Rites of the Egyptians into which he was initiated, from the Mosaic traditions of the Jews, from the Pythagorean fragments of Philolaus, as well as from the numerous instituted Mysteries of the Greeks.

Having returned to Athens, Plato established his school in the Academy, a wooded place of exercise in the suburbs of the city. It was from this Academy that his school secured its name. The wooded grove was not a healthy place and Plato on at least one occasion came near death, being ill for eighteen months because of the unwholesomeness of the air. His physician advised him to move his school but Plato refused, declaring it to be more philosophic to lift himself to a state of physical and mental wellbeing by which he could be immune to the evils of the place. In this, he succeeded and suffered no more. Over the entrance to his school, he placed the words: "Let none ignorant of geometry enter here." By geometry was inferred the whole science of universal mechanics.

In addition to the journeys already mentioned, Plato made three voyages to Sicily, the first when he was about forty years old. This was to study the eruption of Mt. Ætna and to perfect his knowledge of astrology. It was on this journey that Plato was sold into slavery through the machinations of Dionysius, Prince of Syracuse. On this occasion, one Anniceris of Cyrene purchased his freedom. Later, when Plato's friends sought to repay this debt, Anniceris would not accept the money. The funds were therefore used to buy the garden of the Academus. Plato's Academy is sometimes called the first university in history.

Plato continued quietly in the Academy, and although writing frequently on political subjects, in no way taking part in public affairs. His fame greatly spread and disciples came to him not only from nearby cities but from distant countries. He never married and bequeathed his estate to a son of his second brother. He died in the 13th year of the reign of King Philip of Macedon, in his 81st year, on the same day whereon he was born. It was said of him that he died at the most venerable of all ages, "having completed the most perfect number of years, namely 9 multiplied by itself." He died of no disease but simply of old age, which Seneca declares was the reward of his temperate and diligent existence. He was found dead with the books of Sophron lying under his head.

PLATO

Plato derived his philosophical inspiration from a variety of sources. Knowledge came to him not as a revelation but through an unfoldment of the reasoning powers within himself. The remote source of his knowledge was the Orphic Mysteries which were brought to Greece from Asia nearly 1000 years before the birth of Plato. The Orphic Mysteries were an elaborate metaphysical system and the deep truths which Orpheus had taught at the dawn of Grecian civilization exerted a powerful influence on nearly all the schools of philosophy and religious thought which developed and flourished in the Hellenic states. Without a knowledge of the Orphic Mysteries, it is impossible to interpret the more profound aspects of Plato's thought. His gods were the Orphic divinities, and the whole framework of his metaphysical system was derived from the sublimity of the Orphic conception.

Plato was also deeply indebted to the disciplines of Pythagoras, the sage of Samos. Pythagoras, the first philosopher, had been dead over one hundred years, but fragments of his philosophy were rescued from the ruin of his school. These fragments Plato studied assiduously. He made the Pythagorean lore his own. It has therefore been said that, although the two men never met, Plato was a legitimate disciple of Pythagoras. Plato drew particularly upon the mathematical and numerological philosophy of Pythagoras, attributing numbers to the divine principles, and recognizing deity as the. Supreme Geometrician.

From Socrates, Plato gained immeasurably, especially in logic and ethics. The great Athenian Commoner was a man of practical and utilitarian mind and did much to preserve the balance of Plato's intellect. In this late day it is difficult to tell how much of Plato and his philosophy is present in the Socratic Dialogues, for we have no record of the teachings of Socrates except those recorded in the words of Plato.

Not satisfied until he had made all knowledge his province, Plato traveled extensively, associating himself with several of the most eminent scholars of his time. His travels were not as extensive as those of Pythagoras, but his mind was less obscure in its wordings and no man has done more towards the cultural enlightenment of the race. The Platonic philosophy may be regarded as a summary of the best and noblest in Greek thought, but it should not be accepted as a mere compilation. Everywhere throughout his writings is evidence of a master intellect digesting, assimilating and arranging, so that all ideas become part of One Idea, and all knowledge becomes part of one magnificent summary. Plato was an inclusive thinker, the finest type of mind the race has yet produced. He synthesized the arts, sciences, philosophies and religions, uniting them all and forming from their compound the enlightened man's philosophy of life.

Those who followed after him in the Academy never equaled his vision or his strength. After his death the school broke apart, a considerable number of disciples moving to the Lyceum where they remained under the guidance of Plato's greatest disciple Aristotle. Whereas Plato was of large heart and great body, Aristotle was in every way the opposite, an excellent mind but of critical disposition, angular, thin, and of melancholy body. Plato always referred to Aristotle as the "mind" of his school. On one occasion when Aristotle was absent from a class, Plato looked around remarking, "What? the intellect is not here!" Plato greatly admired Aristotle and was himself too noble to be annoyed by the younger man's constant argument.

For the first twelve centuries of the Christian Era, Plato dominated the philosophy of Christian nations, being generally accepted among even the most bigoted religious communities. In the 13th century, Aristotle came to the fore and for over 300 years usurped the place formerly held by his master. The dawn of modern science still showed the influence of Aristotelian thought, but as the mind of man grows richer with experience, arguments give place to understanding, and Plato will in time be restored to his high place in the admiration of mankind.

After the death of Plato and the increasing power of Aristotle, the Platonic doctrines decreased in influence and finally ceased in Greece, to be restored in the 3rd century of the Christian Era by the Neo-Platonists of Alexandria. For 200 years Platonism flourished again. Such great men as Proclus and Plotinus revealed the luster and grace of Plato's philosophy. The increasing power of Christianity destroyed the Alexandrian culture, depriving Platonism of its religious influence, so that it became a way of thinking rather than a doctrine or system of belief. It has remained so until this day, its political and social inferences taught, and to a great measure appreciated, but its spiritual and metaphysical part ignored and rejected. Platonism is not only a philosophy; it is a religion. It is a way of thinking, a way of living, and a complete spiritual institution.

Plato's philosophy surrounds the principle of Unity. To him, the concept of Unity was all-pervading, everywhere present and evident. Division was an illusion. To accept a philosophy of division was ignorance. Unity was reality and the doctrine of Unity was truth. Ignorance sees many separate things in the world; wisdom sees only the many parts of one thing. God, man and the universe are related fragments of a common unity. This concept is true monotheism, for monotheism is more than admitting the existence of one God—it is the realization of the existence of one life of which all living things are part. All learning, then, is the study of relationships. It is not the analysis of isolated natures, but rather it is the coming to understand the part that each play in the drama of the Whole.

Plato's concept of God is moral rather than physical. To him, God is Truth, the fact or the reality which sustains the universe. Unity or oneness is the evidence of truth, even as law is the evidence of intelligence. Whatever truth does must be unity or one-ness, for truth cannot be the parent of diversity. What we call diversity is merely an infinite process in unity, which we do not understand. Plato acknowledged no principle of evil. What appears to be evil is only a form of truth that we cannot understand—a single circumstance which we have not been able to fit into the general plan because of the inadequacy of our own understanding. Truth, being not merely mechanical fact but rather living fact, is the spiritual principle that animates all living creatures. Thus, there is truth in everything. To discover the truth in the universe and the truth in self—these are the duties of such as desire to be wise.

The universe is a manifestation of truth. Truth, unfolding, causes to emerge from its own being relative truths in distinction to their source—Absolute Truth. Relative truths are the gods, the sustainers of the world. From them issues the formal universe, sustained by relative truth. Men are the progeny of the gods, inwardly composed of Absolute Truth (spirit) and outwardly composed of relative truth is varying degrees (soul, intellect, body). The inward nature of man, being in itself of greater virtue than the body, is referred to as the superior part and abides in the heart. The intellect, being the next in the scale of values, dwells in the brain, which the Platonists call the Acropolis of the body. The emotional and animal propensities, the least permanent parts of man, are again in a lower place, and man becomes thus an empire composed of parts. These parts, however, are all conditions of one divine Principle. As the body is united in action, so it is united in the source. The ignorant man is in servitude to his animal nature; the partly informed man is in servitude to his intellectual nature; and the divinely enlightened man is united with his spiritual principle, which is the sustaining power in the midst of his being.

The ancients generally used the term "world" to signify what we call the universe, that is, creation, or the whole out-pouring of subjective energy into objective form. He does not conceive, however that the "world" is eternal, therefore he does not apply to it the term "being" in as much as "being" cannot be qualified by a concept of beginning and end. On the other hand, the world is not an illusion. He cannot say of it that it is "not-being." Therefore, asks the Platonist, what is it? And Plato replies that it is suspended between being and not being and is therefore properly termed "becoming." This is the concept of eternal growth. All progress is part of the process of becoming. This is the concept of eternal growth. Plato was an evolutionist. Things are never born, they never die, but they always change. This changing is on an ascending scale. Things are never less than they are—all change is growth. What is growth? Growth is the unfoldment of inner truth, a process as eternal as truth itself. Plato therefore visions vast cycles of time, inconceivable to human reason, but necessary to the hypothesis of eternal growth. Of course, it is not forms that grow. It is life growing through forms. In the universe this is evolution, in man it is reincarnation. Plato believed in Reincarnation, and taught it as the only reasonable solution to the mystery of human life.

In the last few years, there has been considerable discussion of Plato's political theories. During his lifetime Plato remained entirely aloof from politics but he could not fail to consider the political corruption that weighed heavily upon society even in his own time. Plato sensed that education alone could bring an end to the social evils of the race. He believed that this education must have its beginning in earliest childhood. He knew only too well that inadequacy of viewpoint led to those shortsighted evils which corrupt the state and destroy nations. He realized that all men are not fitted for a high degree of spiritual realization, but he reasoned that the state is not ruled by all men but by a small group of men who lead and direct the destiny of the rest. He knew that the men who lead must know and understand. If these men lack vision, then all the nation must perish. From these realizations, Plato evolved his system of government by the philosophic elect. His ideal state was that in which wise men protected and instructed the uninformed, recognizing leadership as a responsibility and an opportunity for exploitation. How clearly the centuries have shown the rightness of his viewpoint. We have tried in a thousand ways to avoid the adoption of Plato's government. So-called substitute after substitute has failed for the reason that there can be no substitute for truth. We must say that Plato's plan is social rather than political. It would transform states or nations into social orders, removing the political interference, and establishing government as community service and community cooperation.

Plato's theory of education differs widely from our present concepts. He envisioned the state as the teacher of its own people. Religion, science, art, literature, and all the cultural parts of knowledge together constituted the state. Spiritual as well as physical education was the natural birthright of the citizenry, and the state itself was these things. The temple was the city hall, and around this central axis of philosophical enlightenment the community rotated, all the life and industry of the people being geared to this central motif. Instead of political creeds, men should have philosophical creeds. Allegiance should be to principles and not to parties. The good of the whole should be the end to which each individual labors.

This concept was the natural outcome of Plato's doctrine of unity. Men should not work under the illusion that their lives and purposes are separate one from the other, but with the realization that the accomplishments of each are part of the accomplishments of all. Civilization is community existence and community inter-dependence, and civilization requires a standard of mental unfoldment by which each citizen perceives the common good and cooperates towards its accomplishment.

From Socrates Plato derived his understanding of the three-fold nature of truth, that this sovereign reality manifests through three conceivable attributes which Socrates termed: the One, the Beautiful, and the Good. By the One Plato interpreted Unity, the principle which sustains the world. By the Beautiful Plato interpreted Harmony, the mingling of persons or principles to a common good. By the Good Plato interpreted the intrinsic nobility, the rightness and integrity which is the only sufficient and appropriate standard of community action. These also became the criteria of conduct. Whenever a man performed an action, he examined it for its intrinsic value by asking himself, "Is it in harmony with unity, beauty and virtue?" If it cannot pass this test, it is unworthy of a philosopher.

THE PLATONIC DISCIPLINES

As an initiate of the Eleusinian and Dionysian Rites, Plato was not permitted to disclose the secrets of human regeneration communicated to neophytes in the Adita of the temples. Even in his own time he was accused of veiling too thinly the divine Arcana. Throughout Plato's writings, are hints of secret knowledge and allusions to mysteries concealed from the profane. Plato taught that truth and life are intrinsic to spiritual natures but not to the lower elementary parts of man and nature. Lower forms participate in the virtue of truth but do not possess truth in themselves.

For this reason, forms are not in themselves conscious or aware but rather have consciousness and awareness bestowed upon them by the proximity of higher natures. To the degree that man addicts himself to the illusions and intemperance's of form, to this degree he departs from participation in the virtues of divine natures.

The Platonic disciplines may be summed up in the teaching that man shall first realize the reality of truth, and, having accomplished this realization shall then strive with every part of his being to become one with this truth so that every thought and action shall bear witness to integrity and virtue. The Platonists recognize three orders of beings dwelling together in the ample nature of truth, and participating in various degrees in its effulgency. The first order is the gods, in whom truth is most perfectly manifested. The second order is the heroes, enlightened men who, having lifted themselves above ordinary human estate, have become a race of demigods less than divine but more than mortal. The third order embraces mankind and the rest of the diversified material creation, forms in which the divine principle is latent or so slightly awakened as to be incapable of dominating courses of action. "The body," says Plato, "is the sepulcher of the soul." All creatures in whom the higher nature is in servitude to the bodily impulses are properly termed dead, inasmuch as truth is dead within them, having no way of manifesting itself.

The purpose of philosophical education is to release the indwelling integrity so that it may practice dominion over the inferior and unenlightened instincts. Plato writes that learning is remembering. By this he not only means that education rescues from the subconscious mind of the individual the wisdom and experience of previous lives, he also means that through education the memory of Self is released, the divine origin is once more discovered by the intellect, and man comes to know the origin, purpose and destiny of himself. The Platonic approach to philosophy is educational and cultural. Through the sciences, man perfects the reason, and through the arts he refines the passions. Socrates was by profession a sculptor, and his art influenced his philosophy. He taught Plato that the wise man carves out his destiny, perfecting himself as a stonecutter perfects a statue. By education man chips off the rough parts of himself, and by an enlightened process of elimination reveals finally the perfect image concealed within the irregular and imperfect mass of uncultivated instincts and emotions.

It was Plato's idea that the more we know of everything, the more we know about ourselves. Increased knowledge brings increased perspective, bestows greater appreciation, and we honor the universe by understanding it. An ignorant man cannot pay tribute to the gods because he does not understand the gods. Only the wise can know and appreciate wisdom and only the perfect are worthy to participate in the glory of truth.

Plato taught most often seated under a tree, his disciples gathered about him on marble benches. He seldom spoke within doors. He accepted only such as coming to him with a certain standard of accomplishment. Disciples had to be recommended by reputable persons, and he would accept none who had disgraced themselves in their communities. He demanded of each a knowledge of geometry and was pleased if astronomy and music were included among the accomplishments of prospective students. He usually spoke for a certain length of time and then invited discussion. His patience and tolerance were great, and he was painstaking in his effort to make sure that his meanings were clear. He usually followed the Socratic method of making the students answer their own questions by drawing knowledge from them by means of an adroit system of interrogation. His disciples frequently took notes, but this was not demanded of them. Abundant opportunity was given for the students to express their own convictions and opinions. Plato is said to have used a system called "persuasion." The truth in each man is likened to a timid creature, hidden and afraid. Plato coaxed this truth out from its deep hiding place so that each disciple should discover this sacred power locked within himself.

Plato demanded a high development of logic, urging his disciples to accept nothing that was contrary to common reason. He abhorred idle speculation and refused to discuss matters which could not lead to some practical product. He was little given to the discussion of fragmentary forms of knowledge and insisted that his disciples should fit small matters into general orders before they were discussed. To the modern student a practical example of the Platonic method would be to say that in matters of thinking Plato took his disciples into high mountain places where, standing aloof, they could look down upon the world. Below them stretched the plains, dotted with cities, towns, and villages. From an elevated and detached position, it was possible to gain that peculiar perspective, which is termed philosophic insight. Having seen the world in perspective the disciple could then go down into the village's without making the mistake of believing that his own small town was the whole of the world. Narrow-mindedness cannot follow upon broad viewpoints.

Plato reasoned from generals to particulars. His generality was truth and his particulars were the innumerable manifestations of intelligence present everywhere in nature. Plato reasoned downward from divine concerns. He discovered the world by discovering God. He estimated all material matters from the standpoint of their divine origins. In this attitude, he was a true metaphysician. Life was the foundation and form of the temporary structure raised upon it. He saw nature as the shadow of the gods. His principal discipline was to instruct others in this perspective that they might also perceive the one divine principle which sustains and nourishes the infinite diversity of temporal forms.

QUOTATIONS

"Rhetoric is the art of ruling the minds of men!"

"Through obedience learn to command."

"Whosoever is delighted in solitude is either a wild beast or a god."

"Poets utter great and divine things which they themselves do not understand."

"It is better to be unborn than untaught; for ignorance is the root of misfortune."

"God is Truth, and light his shadow."

"Self-conquest is the greatest of the victories."

"Those having torches will pass them on to Others."

"Let no man speak evil of anyone."

"God geometrizes, and His government of the world is no less mathematically exact than His creation of it."

"Nothing in the affairs of men is worthy of anxiety."

"Wisdom alone is a science of other sciences and of itself."

"When men speak of thee, live so as nobody may believe them."

"The most important part of education is right training in the nursery. The soul of the child in his play should be trained to that sort of excellence in which, when he grows to manhood, he will have to be perfected."

"As the government is, such will be the man."

"Love is the eldest and noblest and mightiest of the gods and the chiefest author and giver of virtue in life and of happiness after death."

"Of all the things which a man has, next to the gods, his soul is the most divine and most truly his own!"

Sincerely yours,

Manly P. Hall

PORTLAND, OREGON. OCT. 15 1936

Dear Friend,

MOHAMMED, PROPHET OF ISLAM

Mohammed, Prophet of Islam, the "Desired of all Nations'" was born in Mecca on the 23rd of April, A.D. 571, at the hour of the rising of the morning star. He was born into one of the noblest families of Arabia, which traced its genealogy back to the patriarch Abraham. The name of the Prophet's father was Abdallah and his mother was Amina of the family of Zuhra. The parents of the Prophet were of exceptional virtue in strong contrast to the general corruption of their day, and their marriage, the mingling of two noble houses, was a matter of great rejoicing. The shadow of death, however, was present at the nuptials. Abdallah, pressed by the urgency of his business, made a hurried journey to Syria, leaving behind his young bride. He was stridden with a fatal illness on his journey homeward and passed away in Medina. The Prophet was therefore a posthumous child.

The birth of the Prophet was accompanied by signs and wonders. Of these Washington Irving wrote: "His mother suffered none of the pains of travail. At the moment of his coming into the world a celestial light illuminated the surrounding country, and the newborn child, raising his eyes to heaven, exclaimed: 'God is great! There is no God but God, and I am his Prophet.' Heaven and earth, we are assured, were agitated at his advent. The lake Sawa shrank back into its secret springs, leaving its borders dry; while the Tigris, bursting its bounds, overflowed the neighboring lands. The Palace of Khosru, the king of Persia, shook to its foundations, and several of its towers were toppled to the earth."

The time of the Prophet's birth was also remembered because it coincided with the effort made by the Christian chief Abraha to destroy the Kaaba at

Mecca. The Meccans, being outnumbered by their enemies, could not protect their temple. Therefore, they prayed to Allah that he protects his own house. It is reported that before Abraha could enter the city, smallpox broke out in his army, destroying the greater part of his soldiery and he was forced to depart without reaching the Kaaba. According to the custom of Arabia, the infant Mohammed, when but a few days old, was given into the peeping of Halima, a nurse belonging to the tribe of Banu Sa'd. He stayed with Halima until his sixth year, when the nurse returned him to his mother. Soon after the reunion of mother and son, Amina undertook the journey to the tomb of her husband at Medina. The child travelled with her and on this journey was bereaved of his mother, who died upon the way, leaving him an orphan in his sixth year.

The Prophet's father had many brothers, but it was the grandfather Abdul Muttalib, who assumed the guardianship of the boy. When Mohammed was eight, Abdul Muttalib died and Abu Talib, the paternal uncle, took him into his house and heart. There is a legend concerning the childhood of the Prophet to the effect that while he was still an infant, the angel Gabriel, with seventy wings, appeared to him. Opening the breast of the child, Gabriel took out the heart and cleansed it of the black drop of original sin which was supposed to be in every human heart because of the perfidy of Adam. The angel then returned the organ into its proper place in the Prophet's body and bestowed his blessing upon the future teacher.

Mohammed developed the deepest affection for Abu Talib and was his constant companion. When the boy was in his twelfth year, Abu Talib made a long caravan journey to Syria and, after considerable pleading, his nephew was permitted to accompany him. It was this journey which brought Mohammed for the first time into contact with the Christian sects that dwelt in monasteries in remote parts of the desert. Among the Nestorian Christian communities, Mohammed met a strange and mysterious monk, named Bahira. The monk, apparently possessing clairvoyant powers, predicted Mohammed's future and warned Abu Talib to take the greatest care of the young man for God should call him out of the wilderness.

By his twentieth year, Mohammed had established himself as a respected and admired citizen of Mecca. He was given the name of Al-Amin, which meant the trustworthy or the honorable. His judgment had come to be highly valued and his coming greatness was casting its shadow before it. About this time the Meccans decided to rebuild the Kaaba, the cube-like temple which they had consecrated to their pagan faiths. Everything moved along smoothly until the time came to move the black, stone, the aerolite of Abraham which was said to have fallen from heaven and is regarded as one of the most sacred relics in the world of Islam. Each of the important families of Mecca felt that they were privileged to move the stone into its new place, and civil war threatened. At last, a very wise and aged man asked to be heard and recommended that an arbitrator be chosen. He suggested that the first person to appear at the Kaaba on the following day should be given the choice of deciding who should move the stone, and that all the other factions should agree. The families agreed and waited expectantly. On the following morning the first to appear was Mohammed, which circumstance gratified all of the factions for his honesty and wisdom were household words. Mohammed caused a white cloth to be laid on the ground. Picking up the stone himself, he laid it on the cloth, then calling for representatives from all of the families, he bade them each take hold of the cloth all around. In this way, all of the factions carried the stone and harmony was reestablished.

The widow Khadijah, inheriting a considerable business from her deceased husband, chose Mohammed to manage her affairs. The wisdom of her choice was soon manifest, for under his wise and careful management, her fortune was greatly increased, and all of her affairs ran smoothly. Khadijah, well pleased, offered herself in marriage to the young manager, fifteen years her junior, and through this alliance Mohammed became one of the chief men of Mecca, enjoying everything that wealth and position could bestow. Six children were born from the union, four daughters and two sons. Only one, Fatima, the youngest of the daughters, survived their father, and she outlived him by only six months. By another alliance, made later in life, after the death of Khadijah, Mohammed had one other son, Ibrahim. This child died in infancy.

Mohammed, now secure in worldly things, would have lived and died an honored merchant among the Meccans had not another destiny stirred in his soul. The city of Mecca was the center of a decadent and dissolute paganism, the tradesmen of the community exploiting pilgrims and circulating superstitious doctrines about the idols hat and Uzza. Outside of Arabia, things were scarcely better. Christianity was in the throes of church councils and synods, perverting and misinterpreting the words of Jesus. Asia was in an uproar and the reformations of Buddhism were crumbling before the insidious machinations of Brahmin priests. Mohammed longed for the day when men might worship a true faith, freed from superstitions and intolerance, and established upon an ample understanding. More and more religious matters dominated his thought. Khadijah encouraged him in his every effort, never reproaching him for neglecting his business or dissipating her fortune in charity.

He established the habit of retiring each year to a cavern on the side of Mt. Hira and here, in loneliness and sincerity, he cried out his plea that the religions of man might be purified and the ancient faith of the patriarchs be restored. His religious austerities began to take their toll on his physical health. Weakened in body, his heart aflame with his religious enthusiasm, Mohammed waited and prayed through the years, Khadijah watching over him with ceaseless devotion.

It was in the year 609 A.D. in the cave on Mt. Hira that the angel Gabriel appeared to Mohammed in the midst of the night, in the month of Ramadan. The angel held towards Mohammed a long scarf or shawl of silk upon which, traced in mysterious letters, was the first revelation of what was later to become the KORAN. Gabriel ordered Mohammed to read the words upon the silken strip. "But, alas!" said Mohammed "I do not know how to read." Twice again the angel ordered the Prophet to read and twice again the Prophet pleaded that he could not. The angel then read the verses for him, assuring the Prophet that the power to read would be given him that he might bear witness to the Law.

Mohammed hastened back to discuss with Khadijah the vision. He feared at first that some of the evil spirits of the pagan faith were attempting to deceive him. But Khadijah reminded him that his life was above reproach and therefore there was no reason why he should be deceived. Encouraged by Khadijah, Mohammed accepted the revelation and prepared himself for his ministry as Prophet of Islam. Mohammed's long vigils had not only impaired his health, but had brought about a condition which some writers have called "ecstatic swoons." Most of the Suras or verses of the KORAN were written while the Prophet was in a trance-like condition. The attacks which came over him often asserted themselves without warning and he would fall unconscious. On other occasions, he would sit wrapped in blankets with the cold sweat pouring from his face and body, even on the hottest day. While in this peculiar condition, he would speak, and his words were either noted down or else memorized by his small circle of devoted friends. It was in this way that a great part of the KORAN was written, later in life Mohammed told his friend Abu Bakr that every white hair in his beard was a Sura of the KORAN.

The Night Journey of Mohammed to Heaven on the back of Al-Borak. The face and body of the Prophet are concealed, according to the ordinances of Islam.

Khadijah was the first convert to Mohammed's new faith of Islam, a testimony to his sincerity. For some years the Prophet circulated his inspired doctrines quietly and secretly among a few influential persons, for fear that the Meccans who thrived off the superstitions of the time would rise up and exterminate the cult. At last, it was not possible to keep the secret longer. His increasing body of followers demanded public recognition, and he announced his mission, already the head of a powerful faction. The Meccans retaliated with a plot to assassinate the Prophet. It was an ancient law that the city of Mecca was sacred and that blood should not be shed within its walls, but all the factions got together and, acknowledging a common guilt, arranged the details of the plot.

Mohammed, discovering the danger to his life, left the city, fleeing into the desert with Abu Bakr. For three days the fugitives hid in a cave, outwitting almost miraculously the Meccan horsemen who pursued them. The danger passed; Mohammed continued on to Medina, where he joined a well-organized group of his followers. The flight from Mecca to Medina is called "the Hegira" and is the basis of the Islamic chronological system. Mohammed reached Medina on June 28th, A.D. 622 after a journey of eight days.

After the Hegira, the powers of Mohammed steadily increased. The work of the Prophet was consummated with the conquest of Mecca. At the head of ten thousand followers, Mohammed began the march to Mecca on the 10th day of the month of Ramadan in the 8th year after the Hegira. Islam sees in this the fulfillment of the words of Moses: "He came with ten thousand holy ones." (Deut. 33 2). Mohammed entered Mecca with almost no bloodshed, for he had given orders that none should be injured. Through disobedience to his command, it is said that thirteen of his enemies and two of his own followers died in the conquest of Mecca. This could hardly be considered a bloody victory, and substantiates the general insistence of Islam that Mohammed was a prophet of peace and not of war. Mohammed entered Mecca bearing his standard, a banner made of the black veil of his wife. He circled the sacred Kaaba seven times, then ordered the images in it to be cast down. He then rededicated the temple to the worship of the One God, eternal in the universe. The city thus gained new honors. The annual pilgrimage was established and even to this day each year the pilgrims of Islam cross the desert sands to the black shrouded Kaaba, the axis of their faith.

Two years later, in the 10th year of the Hegira, Mohammed led the Valedictory Pilgrimage. It is said that a hundred and twenty-four thousand persons followed the Prophet. Seated upon the back of a great black camel in the courtyard of the Kaaba, Mohammed spoke to his people with the realization that it would be his last journey to the Holy City. His words were repeated so that the most distant listeners might hear them, and the repetitions were like echoes, repeated again and again so vast was the assemblage. "Oh people! Lend an attentive ear to my words; for I know not whether I shall ever hereafter have the opportunity to meet you here." The Prophet then preached to the assembled faithful the virtues and codes of the faith. At the end of the address, Mohammed cried out: "Oh Lord! I have conveyed thy message." And the voice of the multitude rolled back: "Oh Lord! Surely you have."

The Valedictory Pilgrimage completed; Mohammed returned to Medina where he remained until his death in the 11th year after the Hegira. Four years before, an attempt had been made to poison the Prophet. He had however eaten only a small amount of the poisoned food, but his last years were spent in suffering, resulting from the slow inroads of the poison. Mohammed passed out of this life on the 8th of June in the year 11 A. H. (after the Hegira) in his 63rd year. His last words were: "Lord, blessed companionship on High." He was buried under the floor of the apartment in which he died, at the side of the mosque in Medina. It is said that the Prophet's body was buried lying stretched out on its right side, with the right palm supporting the right cheeky and the face turned towards Mecca. With him were also buried Abu Bahr and 'Umar.

To summarize the character of the Prophet, he was generally acknowledged by those who knew him best to be a simple, earnest man, devoid of mannerisms and untouched by the grandeur complex. He marched with his followers, suffering every hardship they endured. He made his own clothes and pegged his own shoes. Considering the time in which he came and the people who received his message, his teachings were constructive and idealistic, pointing to the improvement of morality, the encouragement of study, and the refining of human relationships. Mohammed is frequently criticized for promulgating the doctrine of polygamy, but it should be remembered that this was the custom of his people, which derived from the authority of Abraham, Jacob, David and Solomon. Mohammed was married to Khadijah at the age of twenty-five. She remained his only wife until the 3rd year of the Hegira when she died. Mohammed was married to Khadijah for twenty-five years. He never recovered from his grief over her loss, and no other ever held the place in his heart or life equal to hers. After the Hegira the Prophet formed other matrimonial alliances principally for political reasons, being the custom of his time. Of those with whom he was associated, Aysha, daughter of Abu Bakr, was the only one who had not been previously married. The attitude of Mohammed himself was to encourage monogamy, and according to the laws he set down the most that a man could have was four wives or consorts. Among those with whom he formed alliances, were several widowed persons whom he married simply to protect. There is no evidence that Mohammed at any time during his life was addicted to any indulgence of any kind, his life being one of austerity and asceticism. Mohammed has also been maliciously misinterpreted in his attitude towards the state of woman after death, for it is clearly set forth in the KORAN that there is no inequality between the sexes in the eyes of God.

THE DOCTRINES OF MOHAMMED

It is generally conceded by authorities on the Islamic cult that the doctrines of Mohammed were largely influenced by Jewish tradition. He drew heavily upon the laws and statutes established by Moses and the other prophets of Israel, and nearly all of his legislations were influenced by the institutions of Jewish law. His religion grew up in a land where three religious systems were influencing the private and public life. Judaism, Christianity and Arabian paganism, the latter a worship of the stars, spirits and demons, all vied for the favor of the populace. That corruption had undermined each of these faiths must be conceded. Arabia was afflicted with innumerable decadent cults, superstition and imposture ridden. It was the evil of the time which produced the Prophet. The nobility of his own mind revolted against the iniquities of the perverted faiths.

The cosmogony which lies behind Mohammed's concept of the universe was similar to that which the Jews derived from the Chaldeans. The concept was geocentric and Ptolemaic. Above the earth and surrounding it were the seven heavens, the orbits of the planets, and beyond these the Empyrean or supreme heaven, the abode of God. There was a gate in each of the orbits of the planets, thus the approach to Deity was up a ladder of seven symbolic rungs, as in the Greek and Persian Mysteries. The whole conception is almost identical with that set forth by St. John in the Revelation. The Mohammedan paradise, a sphere of esthetic ecstasy, was located in the seventh heaven, below the footstool of God, and here were congregated the believers and those who during life had lived, preached or defended the doctrines of the Prophet. The Creation included not only the hierarchies of angels and men but a race of superhuman beings called Dzinn or Genii of whom many extraordinary tales are told.

According to the teachings of the KORAN, certain animals reached heaven. These were the dog of the Seven Sleepers of Ephesus, the ass that rebuffed Balaam, Solomon's ant, Jonah's whale, the ram of Ishmael, the ass upon which the Queen of Sheba rode and her dove, the camel of Saleb, the ox of Moses, and an animal called Al-Boraff upon which Mohammed ascended to heaven in the Islamic equivalent to the Apocalypse. Occasionally, the ass upon which Jesus' rode into Jerusalem is added or substituted for one of the other animals.

The sacred book of Islam is, of course, the KORAN, derived from the word Koraa which means "that which should be read." The KORAN is divided into 114 sections, which may be termed chapters. They are not numbered and the arrangement of them has been subject to numerous changes. In the heading of each chapter, it is noted at what place the revelation was given, whether at Mecca or Medina. The number of verses in the KORAN is about 6000. The book contains 11,619 words, and the number of letters is 323,015, and among the devotees of the faith it has been calculated with great exactitude how many times each letter is repeated in the whole work. Like the writings of the ancient Jews, it is agreed that there is a Cabbalah in the KORAN, and by the systems Notarikon and Gematria, familiar to scholars of cabbalistic literature, a mystical interpretation can be derived from the work.

The KORAN was written in the dialect of the tribe of Koresh, the most cultured of the Arabians, and it is universally acknowledged among the literary of the faith to be the most perfect and elegant example of Arabic literature. This beauty causes it to be referred to as the permanent literary miracle.

The most important point to be emphasized in the faith of Islam is the absolute unity of God. Mohammed makes no point of distinction between the God of Islam, Christendom and Israel, emphasizing merely that Israel and Christianity have departed from a proper understanding of the nature and power of the One and True God. Islam rejects the Trinity of Christendom, maintaining that the triune concept of God was not justified by the Scriptures but was an interpolation legislated into existence by the councils of the church. To Mohammed, God is forever One and Undivided. Prophets and Messiahs are not personifications or embodiments of God but good men sent by God. With this condition Mohammed accepts the ministry of Jesus, acknowledging him to be a true prophet sent out of God, but denying that Jesus differed from other prophets sent in other ages.

Next to the teaching of the absolute Oneness of the Creator, the most outstanding point in the Islamic faith is its teaching of predestination, or the inevitability of that which will happen. Islam teaches that no man can escape his destiny; that regardless of his efforts, that happens, which is to happen. There are no accidents in the universe. In this teaching Mohammed seems to have sensed the universal laws which enclose man in the structure of inevitables. Fears and regrets are useless, each man must certainly meet his own tomorrow. Predestination is not complete fatalism in the ordinary sense of the word. It is true that a man cannot change that which is written for him in the Book of Life, but what man knows his destiny until he achieves it? It may be that the very struggle to avoid fate is part of the fate itself. A man struggling to escape mediocrity achieves a high estate only to discover in the end that his very struggle accomplished the destiny already appointed for him. The doctrine of predestination ordered life in Islam. Patience, serenity, resignation and a graceful acceptance of all that life gave or withheld—these were the virtues of Islam stimulated and perfected by the doctrine of predestination.

The Mohammedan confession of faith is in substance: "There is no God but the true God and Mohammed is his Prophet." Next, in order to this confession, are the six requisites of acceptance. A follower of the Prophet must first believe in God; second, in the hierarchies and angels; third, in the Scriptures; fourth, in the prophets; fifth, in the Resurrection and Last judgment; and sixth, in the predetermination of good and evil. It can easily be seen from this outline how deeply Islam is indebted to the Jewish and Christian sacred books, for, with the exception of certain emphases, the three programs are identical.

Four duties are demanded of the follower of the Prophet. First, he must practice prayer. Second, he must practice charity. Third, he must fast. And fourth, he must make the pilgrimage to Mecca. Prayer is probably the most important of the living practices of the faith. The true believer must pray five times a day under any and all conditions, barring extreme illness. His voice in the morning and his voice in the night must be uplifted in prayer to the God who dwells in the East and in the West and in all the secret places of the world. There are two forms of the practice of charity. First a stipulated amount demanded for the common good, and second voluntary contributions determined by emergencies of the hour. Gifts may be of five things; of cattle or live-stock, of money, of corn, of fruit, or of wares that are sold.

Mohammed referred to fasting as the gateway of religion, and an early prophet called it one-fourth part of the faith. Fasting included not only abstinence from food but the restraining of all the senses and "the fasting of the heart from worldly cares." All Mohammedans are required by the laws of the KORAN to fast the whole of the lunar month of Ramadan, that is, they may not take food during the daytime of that month, and the fast is declared broken if they so much as smell perfumery. The rites of fasting appear in many primitive religions and are salutary dispensations against the intemperance's of semi-civilized peoples. Through associating fasting and bathing with religion, the physical well-being of the race was naturally increased.

The last of the prescribed duties was the pilgrimage to Mecca, and even in this late day it is the great moment in the life of the pious believer. To die without visiting Mecca is almost as serious an offense as to die an unbeliever. Of course, in the days when the members of the faith were limited to Arabia the pilgrimage was possible to nearly all of Islam, but now with believers scattered over the whole surface of the earth the literal fulfillment of the admonition to pilgrimage is impossible of accomplishment. Many thousands of pilgrims visit Mecca every year, but the millions that make up Islam cannot go there. But such as do accomplish the perilous journey, though bankrupt in financial matters, are highly honored in their communities and wear a twist of green voile about their fezzes that all the world may know they have visited the shrine of their faith.

The laws instituted by Mohammed, though actually a part of the faith, are not generally included in a survey of its religious elements. These laws were greatly in advance of those which they displaced, and those regulating industry and calling for the cooperation towards mutual betterment might be profitably studied by nations not of Islamic persuasion even in this late day. The laws regulating marriage and divorce, laws establishing punishment for criminals, laws administering public office—all these the Prophet had to formulate, apply and in some cases revoke where the experiments were not successful. It cannot be denied that in the main these laws elevated Arabia, bringing civilization and culture with them.

One of the most extraordinary legends in connection with Mohammed is the story of his "Night Journey to Heaven." In the midst of the night, as the Prophet lay asleep in Mecca, the angel Gabriel appeared before him and awakened him. After purifying the heart of the Prophet, Gabriel caused a strange animal to appear. This creature, which was called Al-Borak, was a white animal resembling a horse with a human head, and the tail of a peacock. The Prophet mounted upon the back of Al-Borak and was carried in an instant to Jerusalem and the Rock Moriah. After dismounting from the strange animal, Mohammed beheld a ladder of golden rungs that had fallen from heaven. Climbing up the rungs, Mohammed passed through seven gates at each of which stood one of the prophets of patriarchs. At the first gate stood Adam, at the second John, at the third Joseph, at the fourth Enoch, at the fifth Aaron, at the sixth Moses, and at the seventh Jesus. Passing through the gates, Mohammed was brought into the presence of God, but the face of Deity was veiled with thousands of veils. Even so obscured, the brilliance nearly destroyed the Prophet.

This vision gives a rather comprehensive view of the Islamic theory of the universe. Legends abound and traditions are without end, but beneath each of them is some mystical significance if studied and understood by the devout.

After the transition of the Prophet mystical sects sprang up to perpetuate the metaphysical interpretation of the KORAN and the traditions. Chief among these sects was that of the Dervishes. This order still wields considerable influence in the Moslem world. Another mystical movement of great significance is the Sufi. These metaphysical organizations show beyond doubt that in its inner parts the faith of Islam shares the common heritage of metaphysical secrets.

No portrait or likeness of the Prophet Mohammed has descended in the tradition of Islam. His tomb is a place of pilgrimage and a few relics are cherished in some of the more important mosques. It was against the wish of the Prophet that his followers should ever cast a likeness of him, therefore to this day only tradition survives to describe him. He is usually described as a large, well-built man with majestic manner and long beard. There is a tradition that his beard was red or auburn. From the time of its inception, Islam patronized arts and sciences. It encouraged knowledge and culture and preserved some of the best of classical literature through the dark ages of Europe's obscuration. Arab culture came into Europe through Spain and for some time universities at Granada and the Alhambra were the leading educational institutions of Europe. It is recorded by the Moors that they built the first university for the education of women. Arab scientists have contributed much to modern learning, including the Arabic numerals now in common use, the science of algebra, and the earliest experimentation in optics. Modern Islam, mingling its course with the life of the whole race, occupies an honorable place among the religions and beliefs of mankind.

QUOTATIONS

"If I had two coats, I would sell one and buy white hyacinths for my soul."

"The revelation of this book, there is no doubt thereof, is from the Lord of all creatures. Will they say, Mohammed hath forged it? Nay it is the truth from thy Lord, that thou mayest preach to a people, unto whom no preacher hath come before thee."

"He (God) knoweth that which entereth into the earth, and that which issueth out of the same, and that which descendeth from heaven, and that which ascendeth thereto; and he is with you, wheresoever ye be: for God seeth that which ye do. His is the kingdom of heaven and earth; and unto God shall all things return. He causeth the night to succeed the day, and he causeth the day to succeed the night; and he knoweth the innermost part of men's breasts."

"Is it not true, that I came in your midst while you were misguided; so, Allah guided you to the right path. You were indigent; Allah made you prosperous. You were ever at daggers drawn with one another; Allah created mutual affection in your heart."

"You must know that every Moslem is the brother of every other Moslem. You are all equal, enjoy equal rights and have similar obligations. You are all members of one common brotherhood. So it is forbidden for any of you to take from his brother, save what the latter should willingly give."

"You have certain rights over your wives, and so have your wives over you * * * They are the trust of God in your hands. So you must treat them with all kindness."

Yours sincerely,

Manly P. Hall

LOS ANGELES, CALIF. NOV. 1936

Dear Friend,

QUETZALCOATL

At some remote time, a great Initiate-King arose among the civilizations of Mexico and Central America. It is impossible at this late date to determine the period during which he lived, but it is safe to say that it was some centuries before the Christian era. Among the people of the Valley of Mexico this Initiate-King was called Quetzalcoatl which means the Feathered Snake, while further south he was called Kukul-Can a word of similar meaning. Other appellations were also bestowed upon him. He was spoken of as Ehecatl, the Air; Yokcuat, the Rattlesnake; Tohil, the Rumbler; Nanihehecatl, Lord of the Four Winds; and Tlauizealpantecutl; Lord of the Light of Dawn. The heavens and the stars belonged to him, and all the motions of the universe were under his dominion. He was the master of the winds and of the clouds, and the protecting genius of his people.

Modern archeologists at work in the Central American area attempt to prove that Kukul-Can lived in the 9th or 10th century of the Christian era contemporary with Kubla-Khan, warlord of the Mongols. This hypothesis is untenable when we realize that the mask of Kukul-Can, his symbols and the protective snake, are found upon the most ancient of the Mayan and Toltec ruins. It is our opinion that the first Quetzalcoatl or Kukul-Can was a god or king of the Atlanteans whose worship was brought to the Western hemisphere by the fugitives from the Atlantean cataclysm, having established themselves in the Western hemisphere, the progenitors of the Mayans and Toltecs, perpetuated the mythological systems of their submerged empire, preserving among their traditions the esoteric, magical rites of Quetzalcoatl.

As centuries passed, new heroes rose among these people. It is possible and probable that some of the greatest of these heroes might be regarded as incarnations of Quetzalcoatl and were permitted, as a special honor, to assume his name and mask, even receiving worship as the embodiment of the divinity. Ample precedent for such a conclusion may be found in the Greek tradition of Orpheus, the rites of several of that name now being generally confused; or again, the Egyptian Hermes, the Persian Zoroaster, and the Indian Buddha, Gautama being the twenty-ninth of the royal line of sages to bear the same distinguishing title.

If we accept this possibility that the word Quetzalcoatl now signifies a descent of persons bound together by tradition and achievement, it meets most of the needs of the present dilemma. It is also quite possible that the last upon whom wets conferred the sacred name was some great soldier or statesman living in the 9th or 10th century of the present era, whose late achievements are confused with the legends of his predecessors.

As in the case of Zoroaster, there are several different accounts of the life and final departure of Quetzalcoatl. These accounts are almost certain to be merely the lives of the different Quetzalcoatl's. The composite being formed of these different stories is miraculous indeed. Beneath the legends, however, is a certain amount of fact. Dimly, through the contradictions and lesions in the records, may be perceived a great and noble man, founder of a wide-spread faith, a high priest of sacred mysteries, a scientist, a mystic and a philosopher.

Quetzalcoatl was a name to conjure with from the Southern borders of the United States to the highest peaks of the Andes. His mystery cult was served by a hierarchy of priests who termed themselves "serpents" and by virtue of their rituals of consecration partook of the very nature of the god himself. The Initiates of the Quetzalcoatl cult, according to de Bourbourg, referred to themselves as the Sons of the Snake. There is also reference to a subterranean passageway which leads to the "roots of heaven" This passage was called "the Snake's Hole" and only a serpent could enter it. Here is occult symbolism in no uncertain terms. That the serpent hole which leads to heaven is only for such mortals as have become "snakes" is equivalent to the statement in the Old Testament that the mysteries of God are only for the initiates.

It was customary among ancient people to conceal the elements of their philosophical doctrines under mythical adventures ascribed to the hero-god who was the personification of the whole mystical system. The legends of Hiawatha are of such origin, as well as most of the stories concerning Jesus, Buddha and other great World Teachers. The legends of Quetzalcoatl are no departure from this well-established rule. In his birth, life and death we have all the elements of a cosmic myth, skillfully treated, with definite emphasis upon the theogonic and astronomical aspects.

QUETZALCOATL

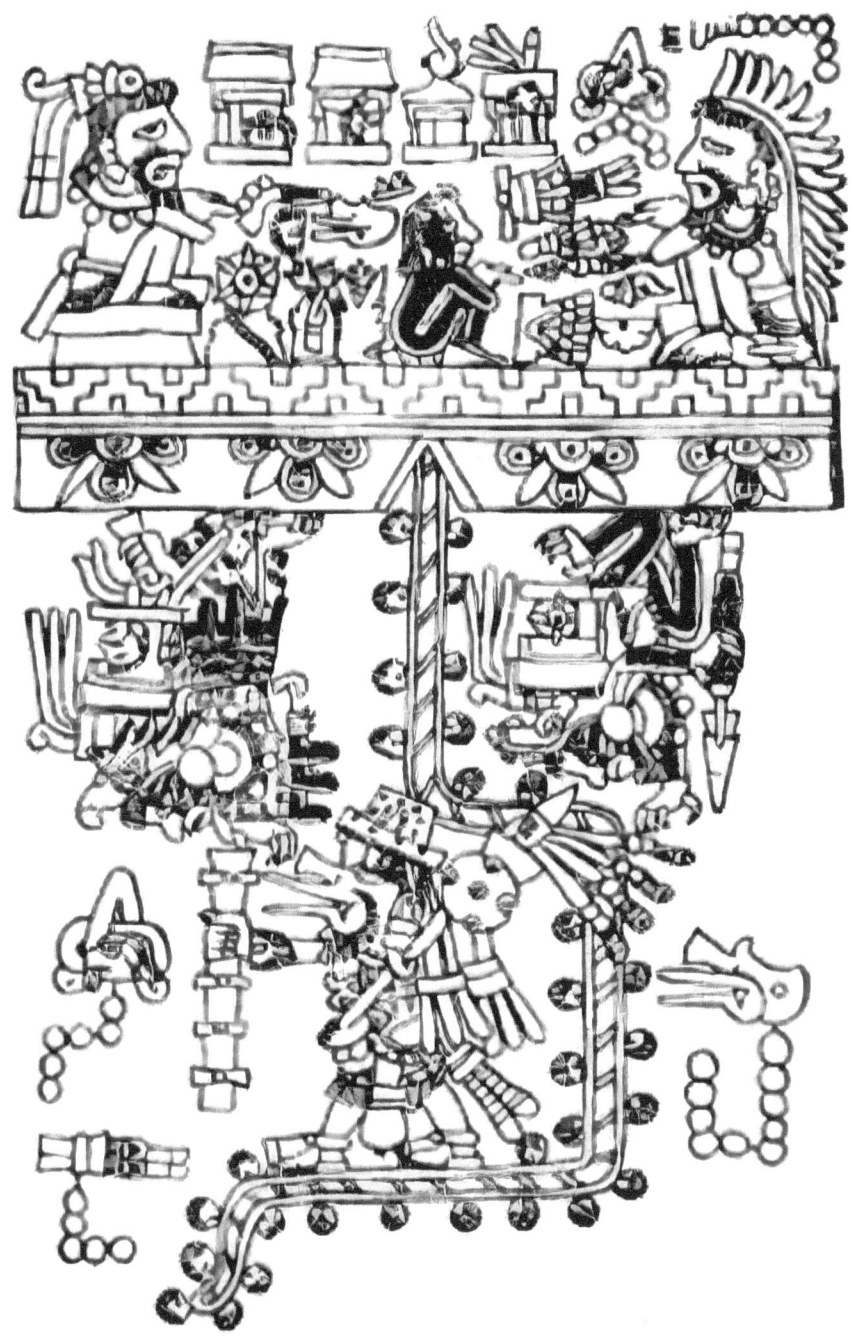

QUETZALCOATL DESCENDING FROM HEAVEN ON A LADDER OF THIRTY-THREE RUNGS.

As Quetzalcoatl is frequently referred to as the patron god of the Toltecs, it would seem appropriate to examine the beginnings of these people. To show how obscure the subject really is we find serious debate as to whether such a race ever actually existed. Those opposing the historicity of the Toltecs declare that the accounts of these people are so mixed up with astronomical cycles that the whole tradition should be regarded as entirely mythological and related to some previous state of man in the heaven world or possibly to the progression of the planets in constellations. Those affirming the reality of the Toltecs declare them to be one of the earliest migrations of the Nahua stocky which moved southward into the Valley of Mexico from the mysterious land of Aztlan, "the place of the reeds" which is the meaning of the word. We have seen a Mexican drawing of Aztlan, which depicts it as an island surrounded by dashing waves, the island itself rising in the middle part of a high mountain. Several legends exist concerning the origin of the Nahua peoples whose sacred land was called Tlapallan which means the country of bright colors. It is also believed they may have come from Chicomoztoc, the sacred seven caverns on the earth. Lewis Spence is of the opinion that these two localities might be New Mexico or Arizona. On the other hand, some of the most authentic traditions point to the fact that Tlapallan could be reached only by water. It has even been suggested that the legends point towards Tabasco as the homeland. It has been connected with Atlantis by some writers, while others believe that Asia was the origin and that those tribes preserved traditions of their migration across Behring Straits by means of canoes. There is an ever-increasing belief in the reality of the Toltec people, but if philosophical facts were known, the whole account might parallel Plato's description of Atlantis, which is a symbolical and allegorical depiction based upon historical circumstances. Facts and fancy have been woven together to serve the purpose of a priest-craft bent on the preservation of metaphysical truths.

According to the historian Txtlilxochitl, the Toltecs founded the city of Tollan about the year A.D. 566. Tollan is now identified with the Mexican city of Tula about 50 miles from Mexico City.

There is a tradition that the Toltecs were led in this migration by a magician who finally, with the aid of divination, selected the spot upon which the great center of empire was to be established. Now, if the Toltec civilization did not arise until the 6th century A.D. it is scarcely probable that it was to these people that Quetzalcoatl came. He would seem to be much earlier, his magical arts already practiced in Mayapan to the South. This leads us to believe that the term Toltec is susceptible to two interpretations. While the term has been given to the first migrations of the Nahuas, it may also apply to the mythological period which preceded historical civilization, a period such as we find recorded as the Golden Age in Greece during which the gods walked with men. While dates and places are hopelessly confused, the astonishing profundity of the Quetzalcoatl story and its correspondences to the mystery rituals of the classical pagan world cannot but awaken admiration and a desire to understand its meaning more clearly.

THE LIFE OF QUETZALCOATL

On a certain day in the mythological country of Tlapallan three sisters were sitting together in their home when there suddenly appeared in their midst a heavenly apparition so fearsome in appearance that two of the sisters died of fright upon beholding it. To the third sister, who seemed strangely calm, the spirit addressed itself, declaring that it had come as an ambassador from the god of the Milky Way to search on earth for a virgin called Chimcdman or Sochiquetzal, who was to bear a son by an immaculate conception and whose name was to be Quetzalcoatl. The tradition then declares that the father of Quetzalcoatl was the great god Ometecutli who is called "the lord of our flesh" and who was the direct creator of mankind. No one apparently has noticed the first two significant letters of this god's name—OM. This can scarcely be a coincidence. The omnific name of the Creator, commences with these two letters in so many of the ancient mystical systems. Here is a definite link with the metaphysics of Asia.

Lord Kingsborough notes the significant fact that the name Sochiquetzal signifies in the ancient dialects "the lifting up of roses" and that in the Islamic traditions concerning the birth of Christ, he was conceived as the result of the Virgin Mary smelling of a rose. In another tradition, the god Ometecutli, who was the personification of the procreative attributes of abstract divinity, is declared to have overshadowed the Virgin Sochiquetzal as an invisible spiritual being, impregnating her with his breath so that Quetzalcoatl was the breath-born son of a divine father and a human mother. Here we have a parallel to Pythagoras whose father is supposed to have been the god Apollo, or Jesus conceived of the Holy Ghost which literally means "spiritual air or breath," and again in the folklore of Britain the magician Merlin whose father was an invisible creature, a fire salamander or dragon and his mother a vestal.

In due time the child Quetzalcoatl was born, his birth being accompanied with the mysterious omens and wonders in the heavens which always accompany a divine incarnation. Some legends affirm that when he entered into terrestrial life, he was already perfect, in wisdom, so that even as a babe he had the reasoning faculties of a man. There are fantastic stories to the effect that he issued into this life wearing his plumed bonnet and adored alike by gods and men. There are accounts that Quetzalcoatl was the youngest of the seven sons of Ometecutli, but the more persistent tradition is that he was the one and only son of his heavenly father and that he came into this world only for a short time to act as a mediator and to reinstate a relapsed humanity in the favor of the heavenly one. The Aztec chronicles state definitely that Quetzalcoatl is the only one of the gods who ever actually possessed the body of a man; all of the other deities were incorporeal, existing in an azonic state like the God of the Christians who is regarded as being everywhere at all times. Thus, Quetzalcoatl fulfills all the requisites of the Platonic definition of a demigod. He is the superman, the link between heaven and earth, who of his own nature constitutes the bridge which connects the two worlds. He is the Son through whom all men must come unto the Father. Quetzalcoatl was born on the day of the seven Canes, and as in the case of nearly all divine children, tradition is silent as to his childhood years. There is a rumor of greatness but no distinct account. At this point, a considerable difficulty arises in an effort to reconcile several legendary accounts. According to some stories, Quetzalcoatl was actually born in Tollan and ruled over that Toltec state as its prince, but the most popular legend declares that he departed from Tlapallan and appeared at Vera Cruz, either riding upon a raft of serpents or being carried in a magical canoe made from the skins of snakes. In appearance, he is generally represented as a man of mature years, even a patriarch with a long beard and fair, white skin. The image of him in the pyramid of Cholula, however, depicts the god as black, bis body adorned with astronomical symbols. When seen upon the raft, Quetzalcoatl was covered from shoulders to feet in a black robe, which was ornamented with a fringe of white crosses. Upon his head was a magnificent bonnet of quetzal plumes and he carried a magic wand with which he performed all those wonders ascribed to Moses' sacred staff. With this wand, he controlled invisible creatures and was continually surrounded by magical forces.

When Quetzalcoatl took over the affairs of the Toltec nation, the people were suffering from droughts and famines so that great distress was upon the face of the land. Knowing that sin was the curse of the fourth age and that the departure of men from the piety prescribed by the divinities was responsible for their tribulation, Quetzalcoatl set himself the task of reordering Toltec culture. Among other things he instituted sacrifices to the gods and revived the interest in spiritual things. His offerings, however, were of no avail until at last he offered his own blood for the redemption of his people. He inflicted several wounds upon his own body and catching the blood in sacred utensils offered it as a covenant to the deities. We remember that Odin, in German, Wotan, wounded himself with his own spear so that he might be qualified to enlighten the world. Both Odin and Quetzalcoatl became gods of thieves even as Christ was crucified with thieves, and one of the names by which Quetzalcoatl was known in the Mexican mysteries was Votan. One of the Spanish authors calls attention to the fact that many of the criminals of Mexico worshipped Quetzalcoatl and Odin was the patron of executed criminals because he voluntarily hung himself from a branch of the Tree of Life. The self-inflicted wounds by which Quetzalcoatl appeased the heavenly wrath were made with sacred thorns, which reminds one of the wreath of thorns. There is most certainly a connection between all of these curious correspondences, but others more startling come to light as we proceed.

At last, to signify that they had accepted the sacrifices and had forgiven the sins of the people, the Toltec gods on their high Olympus, sent a lizard as their messenger to inform Quetzalcoatl that the period of his penance had come to an end. The Valley of Mexico then blossomed as a rose and all good things came to the people. Prescott writes: "During his residence on earth he (Quetzalcoatl) instructed the natives in husbandry and the arts of government. His influence was most benign. Under his tutelage, the people were happy; the air was filled with intoxicating perfumes and the sweet melody of birds. The halcyon days he spent with his people represented to them the Golden Age of Anahuac. At his command, the earth teemed with fruits and flowers, without the pains of culture. An ear of Indian corn was as much as a man could carry. The cotton, as it grew, took, of its own accord, the rich dyes of human art. Wherever he went, all manners of singing birds bore him company, emblems of the whistling breeze." Thus, we see the great magician with a wave of his magic wand re-established paradise upon the earth and over his happy realm he ruled in the capacity of a priest rather than a king.

Concerning the personal life of Quetzalcoatl, contradictions also exist.

Some declare that he was a celibate initiate living in the true manner of a priest, concerning himself only with the spiritual wellbeing of the race; other accounts refer to his consort, Quetzalpetlatl, who is described as the female counterpart or complement of himself. Here we have the Oriental doctrine of shakti's in which each divinity is completed by a female attribute, usually personifying the gentler virtues of the divinity. Even the accounts of the Mayas on the Peninsula of Yucatan agree that it would be a mistake to consider Quetzalcoatl or, to them, Kukul-Can, as a king or temporal ruler. He placed princes upon thrones and defended the dignity of states but remained ever aloof from temporal entanglements, too high and too far removed to enter into the petty disputes of men.

In the Mexican legends of Quetzalcoatl, appear fragmentary bits of significant symbolic lore. We read of the temptation of Quetzalcoatl, how during his penance the spirits of evil came to him and tried to divert him from his course. In another place is the account of his fasting for 40 days, which later became a definite part of the Mexican religious ritual. Then there is the cup which was given to him to drink a mystic sacrament, and one of his many titles was that of "the Morning Star."—Throughout the Toltec mythology he is the Lord of the Eastern Light and must be regarded as a solar divinity as well as a wind spirit. One of his many appellations in the ancient language signifies a vine or the juice thereof. Votan, which means the human heart, was a term sacred to him, and the Mexicans had a ceremony in which they made a model of his body from dough which they baked and then divided amongst themselves and ate with great solemnity. Lord Kingsborough calls attention to the fact that according to the old Jewish prophecies, the Messiah who was to come to Israel was to be of marred or deformed countenance and that his person would be without beauty. Quetzalcoatl fulfils this requirement exactly. Nearly all of the images which have been found of him have been mutilated in the face and those not thus disfigured show the divinity as of the most unprepossessing countenance, usually deeply wrinkled and with a single protruding tooth.

Among the Mayan legends is one to the effect that although Quetzalcoatl was held in high esteem by millions of devoted subjects and followers, he brought down upon himself the animosity of the priestcraft probably because he delivered his people from bondage to the ignorance and superstitions by which these wily sorcerers maintained their own fortune and dignity. They plotted in many ways to destroy him and, at least on one occasion, actually brought him to the sacrificial stone. But his magic seems to have been greater than theirs and he was victorious over his priestly adversaries. The myth of the dying god is certain evidence of the presence of the Mystery ritual. Therefore, we seek in the legend of Quetzalcoatl for this all-important keynote, nor do we need to seek far, for the curious illuminations in the Vatican Codex reveal the whole story. Here are numerous representations of the god crucified and even with curious marks resembling nail wounds in his hands and feet. To quote again from Lord Kingsborough: "The seventy-third page of the Borgian MS. is the most remarkable of all: for Quetzalcoatl is not only represented there as crucified upon a cross of Greek form, but his burial and descent into hell are also depicted in a very curious manner." After forcing the lord of the underworld to pay him homage, Quetzalcoatl rises victoriously from the grave, thus perfecting in every part the mystical system which he had come to institute. At just what period in his life the crucifixion episode took place, we cannot discover, but, as in the story of the crucifixion of Jesus, the elements involved are metaphysical rather than physical and the date would be of no great value.

At this point, the cosmic myth again mingles itself with what may be, at least in part a historical account. We cannot tell just what connection exists between the Golden Age of Quetzalcoatl which crowned the allegorical story of the Toltec civilization, but we do know that the civilization itself, weakened by internal decay and the deterioration of moral fabric, was overthrown by other Nahua tribes led by the sorcerer god, Tezcatlipoca. This demon elected himself the adversary of Quetzalcoatl and determined to break the reign and power of the magician priest. At this point Quetzalcoatl seems to become for at least an instant identical with the Toltec nation itself and Tezcatlipoca and his two fellow conspirators with three tribes of Nahua barbarians. It is said, for instance, that Tezcatlipoca, assuming the appearance of an aged man, gained audience with Quetzalcoatl and, as a physician, prescribed a remedy for an illness which had befallen the aged priest. The medicine which Tezcatlipoca gave Quetzalcoatl was in reality pulque, an intoxicating drink, which benumbed the senses of Quetzalcoatl. The story evidently intends to convey that the evil spirits drugged the Toltec empire and brought about its destruction through dissipation and intemperance.

Quetzalcoatl remained with the Toltecs until his empire was so demoralized by the scheming's and plotting's probably of his political enemies that it was no longer possible to maintain the integrity of the people. Feeling that the task which he had come to accomplish was ended, and that there was no further good which he could accomplish for the Toltecs, Quetzalcoatl departed from Tollan to return to Tlapallan the mysterious "Orient" from which he had come. Departing from the city which he had elevated to dignity, he set out in his very advancing years for Cholula, which was to be his first important stopping place. That his treasures should not fall into the hands of the demon Tezcatlipoca he destroyed the buildings which he had erected, hid his treasures and jewels in caverns over which he caused mountains to appear by magic. With a wave of his wand, in the words of Lewis Spence, he changed the cocoa trees into mesquites and ordered all of the birds of rich plumage and song to quit the valley of Anahuac and to follow him in his pilgrimage. Thus, he left the land as he had found it—a desert—and his curse has remained upon it. His adversaries, seeing that he was rendering valueless the land which they were striving to steal from him, besought him to reveal before his departure the secrets of smelting, of painting and lapidary which he had communicated to his chosen people. But the god refused and continued his journey, preceded by musicians who played soft melodies to cheer his weary footsteps.

In some accounts, it is stated that Quetzalcoatl remained for twenty years in Cholula, others give a much shorter period for his stay. In honor of his presence there, the great pyramid was built. From Cholula, in one account, he continued on to the shore of the Gulf of Mexico where he called to the sea and there immediately appeared above the water the wizard skiff of serpent skins drawn by dragons.

Turning to his followers gathered upon the shore, the aged Quetzcdcoatl made the prophecy that was to prove the future undoing of the Aztec empire. He said that in a later age he would come back and with his descendants establish the fifth great epoch which would bring with it the permanent paradise of which the Eden he had invoked by magic was but a taste. Then, stepping into his ship, he disappeared over the curved mystery of the horizon, returning to his sun-father who had called him back to the fabled land of Tlapallan.

There is also another account of the passing of Quetzalcoatl, which though entirely different also possesses much symbolic interest. In the Aztec mythology is described how the aged prince, Feathered Serpent, after his departure from Cholula, journeyed as far as Coatzacoalcos, where he died full of years and honored for his wisdom. His body was carried in a stately procession to the high peak of Mt. Orizaba, where, as the multitudes gathered about it, was consumed by a divine flame which descended from heaven as in the passing of Zoroaster, the Persian Fire Magus. As the flames surrounded his body, there appeared in the midst of the conflagration a bird of such magnificence that its plumage darkened the flames by contrast. It was the spirit of Quetzalcoatl ascending to heaven in the royal guise of the peacock.

Lewis Spence gives a still different account of the passing of the Feathered Serpent magician. He writes that Quetzalcoatl "cast himself upon a funeral pyre and was consumed and that the ashes rising from the conflagration flew upward and were changed into birds of brilliant plumage: His heart also soared into the sky and became the morning star. The Mexicans averred that Quetzalcoatl died when the star became visible, and thus they bestowed upon him the title 'Lord of the Dawn.' They further said that when he died, he was invisible for four days, and that for eigth days he wandered in the underworld, after which time the morning star appeared, when he achieved resurrection, and ascended his throne as a god."

That certain parts of the Quetzalcoatl legend have an astronomical interpretation is quite evident. The Mexicans had periods composed of what they called the binding of years. These bindings contained fifty-two years and constituted a cycle. According to traditions the end of the world would occur at the termination of one of these fifty-two-year cycles, therefore this period was always marked with greatest solemnity and the new year was announced when the stars of the Pleiades passed the zenith on the fatal day. This passage promised an extension of fifty-two years to the life of the empire and during the period of Aztec supremacy, human sacrifices were offered to propitiate the gods at this time so that they might prolong the duration of the world. Quetzalcoatl remained in Mexico for fifty-two years (one of these binding periods) and, as has already been noted, the Spaniards also arrived on one of these psychological periods. Quetzalcoatl disappeared from the sight of men after the great fifty-two-year festival at Cholula, journeying in the magical direction of all great Initiates—towards the east, his eternal home. Humbolt says that at the end of the fifty-two-year cycle the Aztecs extinguished all their lights, a peculiar ceremony which the Druids performed annually. The Indians also at this period crucified a victim, believing that by this crucifixion, they would gain a respite from the destructive powers of the gods.

FRAGMENTS OF ANCIENT MEXICAN METAPHYSICS

One has but to examine the surviving fragments of Nahutian mythology and history to realize that a high order of metaphysical learning existed among the original Americans. Even Roman Catholic writers admitted that magic flourished among the peoples of Mexico and that the priests and philosophers of that nation were deeply versed in astrology and the necromantic arts. The episode of the arrest and detention of two Aztec sorcerers, accused by the church of attempting to weave spells against the Christian clergy, is especially interesting for even the pious fathers were forced to admit that their prisoners dissolved into empty air before their very eyes—a circumstance which was passed over very lightly. The ill-fated Montezuma was surrounded by seers and prophets who, from signs which appeared in the heavens, warned the emperor that the conquistadores with their horses and guns were not emissaries from the sun-god but plundering mortals with an eye for loot.

Montezuma, being a great prince, was well learned in the lore of his people, and it was this very learning that proved his undoing. The most ancient traditions of his race, perpetuated by the wisest of each generation, declared that the history of the world was divided into five great epochs. These five vast periods were separated from each other by great cataclysms in which great portions of mankind perished. In the codex Vaticanus, it is written that in the first age water reigned supreme until at last it rose up and swallowed all creatures save two who escaped by means of a tree. As the form of a ship appears in this tradition, it is lively that the tree was hollowed out to form a crude boat in which the Mexican Noah and his wife rode safely over the deluge. In this first age, there were also giants and strange monsters with teeth that weighed three pounds each. The second age was that of wind which, by the force of its blowing, finally destroyed the whole world. One man and one woman survived this destruction also by concealing themselves within a hollow stone which was so heavy that the wind could not blow it away. During this period, great masses of humanity were changed into apes. The third age was that of fire and was ended by a terrible outburst of flames which burned up the world. Again, a Noah and his wife were saved this time by seeking refuge in subterranean caverns where the terrible heat could not reach them. The fourth age was that of present humanity and its destruction will be brought about by sin—the sin of man. It is called in the old Codex the age of the black hair. It was in the early centuries of this age that the great race of the Toltecs, under their divine priest-king, Quetzalcoatl, was destroyed by the sorcery of the Nahuas under their demon war-god, Tezcatlipoca. All this Montezuma knew and from the same traditions he had also learned that a fifth age was to come, a golden age in which the gods would return, or more correctly, turn with favor to the Aztec nation through their ministering intermediary, the Feathered Snake.

EXTRACTS FROM AN AZTEC PRAYER

"O, Mighty Lord, under whose wing, we find defense and shelter, thou art invisible and impalpable, even as night and the air. Now can I, that am so mean and worthless, dare to appear before thy majesty? Stuttering and with rude lips I speak, ungainly is the manner of my speech as on leaping among furrows, as one advancing unevenly."

"Yea, what doest thou now, O Lord, most strong, compassionate, invisible and impalpable, whose will all things obey, upon whose disposal depends the rule of the world, to whom all are subject,—what in thy divine breast hast thou decreed?"

"O Lord, all-powerful, full of mercy, our refuge, though indeed thine anger and indignation, thine arrows and stones, have sorely hurt this poor people, let it be as a father or a mother that rebukes children, pulling their ears, pinching their arms, whipping them with nettles, pouring chill water upon them all being done that they may amend their puerility and childishness."

"Let the small birds and thy people sing again, to approach the sun; give them quiet weather; so that they may cause their voices to reach thy highness, and thou mayst know them."

Yours Sincerely,

Manly P. Hall

LOS ANGELES, CALIF. DEC. 1936

Dear Friend,

JESUS

In the Protoevangelium of James, it is written that Joachim was a man of great piety and considerable wealth who devoted his life and his means to works of charity. But when Joachim brought his gifts to the temple Reuben, the high priest, of Israel, reproached him, saying: "It is not lawful for thee to offer thy gifts first because thou hast been the father of no child in Israel." It followed that Joachim, bowed with grief, went forth into the wilderness, fasting and praying for forty days and forty nights. His prayer to the God of Israel was answered. Anna, his wife, conceived and bore a child and when the infant was delivered, the midwife said: "It is a girl," and Anna gave thanks to God and named the babe Mary.

Now Anna had taken a vow that if God granted unto her an issue, she would dedicate it unto the Lord to the service of the sacred house. So, when Mary reached the age of three years, Joachim and Anna brought her to the steps of the temple and the high priest received her as one dedicated to the holy life.

CHRISTMAS GREETINGS
and
BEST WISHES for a HAPPY NEW YEAR

In the years that followed, Mary dwelt in the apartments of the temple and so gentle and charming were her ways that all of the house of Israel loved her. So, things continued until her twelfth year at which time, according to the law, the priests gathered in council to decide her future; it being unlawful that she should dwell longer in the house of God. Now the priests decreed that the high priest should enter into the Holy of Holies and ask of the Lord what should be done with the girl. Zacharias was at that time the high priest and he put upon himself the robes of glory and the breastplate and he entered into the presence of the Lord; and the angel of the Lord spoke unto him, saying: "Go forth and summon the widowers of the people and let them take a rod apiece, and she shall be the wife of him to whom the Lord shall show a sign."

Now Joseph, the Panther, was the most aged of the widowers of Israel and hearing the summons of the priests he laid down his axe and came with the others to the porch of the temple. The priests gave to each man a rod, each with a different marking upon it. The rods were then taken into the temple to be blessed. Afterwards they were distributed again and the last to have his rod returned was Joseph, and as he took hold of the rod, a dove flew out of it.

Joseph was greatly embarrassed, for he had grandchildren as old as Mary and was himself close to ninety years of age. He said to the priests: "Let me not become ridiculous before the children of Israel." But the priests replied that only misfortune could come to one who gainsaid the will of the Lord. So, Joseph took Mary into his house and continued in his trade of a builder.

When Mary was about fifteen years old and had been three years in the house of Joseph, a voice spoke to her as she stood one day drawing water from the well. She could not see where the voice came from and in great fear ran back to the house. As she sat spinning one day, a celestial being appeared, announcing that she should bear a son, that his name should be Jesus, and he should be the savior of his people. And Mary answered, "Behold the servant of the Lord is before him; let it be unto me according to thy word." In the course of time. Joseph learned that Mary was to bear a child and he was sorely troubled and afraid. The angel of the Lord came unto him also and Joseph went to the priests, and the priests doubted and tested Joseph and Mary, but finding them without fault, the high priest said: "If the Lord God hath not manifested your sins, neither do I judge you," and dismissed them.

An order had been issued by Augustus Caesar that a census should be taken of all the people of Israel. It was further decreed that they should come up to Bethlehem to be enrolled. Joseph was deeply troubled for he did not know how to enroll Mary, being ashamed to list her as his wife because of the difference in ages and afraid to register her as his daughter. He finally comforted himself with the thought that the Lord would reveal the way, so he saddled his ass and to one of his sons he appointed the task, of leading it. He placed Mary upon the animal, and following behind started for Bethlehem.

They were about three miles from the city when the time came, for Mary to bring forth her child and Joseph found a cave and it was there that the infant was born. A great light shown in the cavern and gradually the light withdrew into itself and the clouds which filled the place parted and the babe was seen. After three days, they moved to the inn and the hostelry being filled, there was only room in the stable, and the child was cradled in a manger.

From the birth of Jesus, the Gospels take up the story, and, with certain minor points of difference, describe particularly the years of the Ministry, beginning with the Baptism by John and terminating with the Ascension. Little is known of the childhood of the Master. The shepherds pay homage at his crib and wise men, coming out of the East, bring gifts to him. Jesus is taken as an infant to Egypt to escape the wrath of Herod. Later, by inference, he returns to his own country and appears in the synagogue at the age of twelve, arguing with the priests and elders. Again, by inference, it is suggested that he practiced the trade of Joseph at least for a time.

From the Apocryphal Gospels, we gather a few more details, uncanonical but probable. The Gospel of Thomas describes him growing up in the house of Joseph, performing miracles and manifesting even in infancy evidences of extraordinary powers. On one occasion, he molded little sparrows of clay. He clapped his hands and the birds came to life and flew away. Jesus was at that time five years of age. Later he studied with a certain teacher, Zaccheus by name, who soon acknowledged his incapacity to instruct him.

The Gospel of the pseudo-Matthew reports many sayings of Jesus attributed to his childhood years. The Arabic Gospel of the infancy, of a much later date, and highly embellished with the traditions of the first seven centuries of the Christian era, devotes considerable space to the questioning of Jesus by the learned during his twelfth year. In this account, Jesus is examined in theology, philosophy, science and medicine, and is discovered to be completely learned in all these matters. In the 51st chapter of the Arabic Gospel, it relates that Jesus demonstrated his skill as an astronomer, and the inference is inevitable, that he was learned in the mysteries of astrology. From the twelfth year on, little can be discovered from even the Apocryphal Gospels. The Talmud offers a clue. He is said to have visited Alexandria with a certain Rabbi Jehoshua Ben Berachiah.

JESUS AND HIS DISCIPLES FROM A FIFTEENTH CENTURY WOODBLOCK

In Egypt he studied the occult and metaphysical arts, and having mastered certain of the abstruse sciences of the Egyptians, he returned to Syria expounding the doctrines which he had received. From this account, it would appear that Jesus studied in the Hermetic colleges of the Ptolemies. Alexandria was a melting pot of Asiatic and Hellenic cultures. Most of the religions of the known world were represented there and the public mind was remarkably liberal and tolerant. From the priests and philosophers of Alexandria, Jesus could have learned not only the metaphysical arts but the great systems of world philosophy—the proper background for the Ministry.

Edouard Schuré, the distinguished French mystic, associates Jesus with the Essene Order. Earlier writers have also suspected that the references in the Bible to Jesus the Nazarene have been mistranslated and should have read Jesus the Nazarite, that is Jesus of the Order or Society of Nazarites. The Nazarites and Essenes were either branches of the same Brotherhood or else closely associated orders, imposing similar vows and obligations and expounding similar mystical philosophies.

It is quite possible that the historical Jesus was born of parents who were members of the Essene colony of which Josephus wrote with deepest respect. The Essene sect seems to have been founded by Pythagoras. It was certainly of Greek origin and, having been adapted to Syrian soil, flourished particularly in the villages and towns about the Dead Sea, and on Carmell. The doctrines of the society included both Grecian and Egyptian elements, and the order may be regarded as a legitimate Mystery School, bestowing initiation and conferring the arcana. The Essene cult was divided into two distinct groups. The highest consisted of monks and recluses who had renounced all worldliness to live in the caves or monasteries of the Order. The second division consisted of lay brothers and sisters who had taken, vows of purity but still lived in the family relationship, supporting themselves by certain arts and crafts. According to the laws of the Order, these lay brothers and sisters could not engage in any business of bartering or exchange but might follow only such pursuits as were of a simple constructive nature. For this reason, they frequently took the trade of carpentry, pottery or building. Among the symbols of their Order, were builders' tools as in the case of modern Freemasonry. The Essene communities flourished under cooperative economic policies and the lives of the members were devoted principally to learning, teaching, acts of piety, healing and befriending. So well educated were these Essenes, in a time of general ignorance, that Roman officers stationed in the Holy hand frequently engaged them as tutors for their children. Crime was unknown in their midst and they were by far the wisest and noblest of the Jewish sects.

The Essenes were a Messianic sect, looking towards the advent of a promised Messiah who would rise in Israel. Some of their members took the vow that they would cut neither hair nor beard until the "Desired of Israel" should come. It has been suggested that John the Baptizer, seeing Jesus for the first time, recognized him as a holy man because he wore his hair and beard according to the vow of the Nazarite and was also dressed in the raiment of the Order.

Joseph was of the chosen profession of the Essenes—a builder—possibly in the mystical sense rather than in the literal one. This might also explain why Joseph was selected to receive Mary into his house and also why Joseph and Mary were chosen as the guardians of an incarnating adept.

If Jesus was born into an Essene community, his religious education would have begun in infancy. He would have grown up in an atmosphere of gentleness and piety. He would have enjoyed rare opportunities to release the depth and greatness of his own soul. His youth would have been spent in study and travel, and after a proper probationship and having reached the proper year, the age of thirty, could by choice have taken the vows of the initiate and entered the higher division of the Order. In this way the several accounts of his life might be parts of one fact. As an Essene he would have traveled in Egypt, possibly in Greece, and he might even have undertaken the difficult journey to India as did Pythagoras before him. The Mysteries had no religious prejudice and disciples traveled from one school to another, perfecting themselves in the wisdom of all nations and all ages.

In the Homis Monastery in Little Tibet there are said to be manuscripts proving that Jesus joined a caravan bound for India where he remained for some time, returning to Syria in his twenty-ninth year. It is quite possible that records concerning the youth of Jesus were suppressed or destroyed by the early church to prevent members of the new faith from discovering that Christianity was rooted in the religions of the so-called pagans. Unfortunately, the bigotry and fanaticism of a few people is responsible for nineteen centuries of misunderstanding and persecution in Christendom. Hundreds of books were destroyed by the Council of Nicaea and among them may have been the records of the childhood and training of Jesus.

The Ministry of the Master which followed upon the Baptism by John continued for less than three years. The Ministry was devoted to two principal lines of activity—the performing of miracles and the teaching of the New Covenant, usually translated as Testament. By the miracles Jesus is made to appear as a wonder-worker like the fabled Mahatmas of Asia, and by his teaching, he is made to appear as a reformer of the corruptions which had arisen in the orthodox Jewish faith. He states definitely that he has come not to tear down the faith of Israel but to fulfill it and to bear witness to that which had been prophesied by the patriarchs.

Like most great teachers, Jesus could not ignore the social problems of his day. Jerusalem, the city of the prophets, Judea, the land of the patriarchs, was in bondage to Rome. Numerous groups had sprung up among the Jews, praying, plotting, and planning for deliverance. Jesus could scarcely fail to be involved in the political problems of his people. Philosophers are not politicians, but nearly all great philosophers have realized that the perfection of mankind cannot be accomplished without certain reforms in the social and political state of humanity. Jesus soon drew about him followers and disciples who visualized the teacher not only as a man of God but as the political liberator of their nation. From various walks of life Jesus chose twelve disciples of the first order, and it is also related seventy-two others who formed a second circle. These disciples and followers, in their enthusiasm, contributed to the destruction of that which they loved most. Through their religious non-conformity, they alienated the Jewish priests, and through the political inferences of their message they alienated the Roman governors. All that remained was the common people—a force easily molded by ulterior motive.

As the years of the Ministry drew to a close, Jesus and his little band of followers were drawn fatally and inevitably to the city of Jerusalem. Jesus realized that the end was near, but the message had to be brought to the city of the Kings, the very heart of Israel. Misunderstood most by those closest to him, Jesus gathered them about him for the last time in fraternity and celebrated the Passover with the Last Supper. There was much more to this sacrament than is preserved in the Gospels. It was the last secret meeting of the twelve who were to carry on after the passing of their Master. Of these twelve, only one died a natural death. Judas, it is said, destroyed himself, and all of the others except St. John were martyrs. It is said that the disciples and the Master sang together and St. Augustine, in the 236th letter to Bishop Ceretius, preserves the words of the song:

"I wish to unbind, and I wish to be unbound.

I wish to save, and I wish to be saved.

I wish to beget, and I wish to be begotten.

I wish to sing; dance ye all with joy.

I wish to weep; be ye all struck with grief.

I wish to adorn, and I wish to be adorned.

I am the lamp for you who see me.

I am the gate for you who knock.

Ye who see what I do, do not tell what I am doing.

I have enacted all this discourse. And l have not been in any way deceived."

The hymn was followed, in the ancient Jewish custom, by the breaking of the bread and the passing of the cup. After this, according to one of the Apocrypha, Jesus and his Apostles celebrated the Mystery with a ritualistic dance, after which certain matters were discussed which might not be revealed to the profane. The Last Supper took place on Wednesday, the last day of April, in the evening.

In a sense the Last Supper concludes the Ministry. The Master has put his house in order, has finished the communication of such arcana as he gave to his disciples. The only hint that we have as to the nature of the secrets which Jesus imparted are to be found in the Gnostic Gospels, the Pistis Sophia and the Books of the Savior.

The Garden of Gethsemane follows. The suffering man appears briefly through the otherwise tranquil tradition. The arrest of Jesus follows. He is brought before both Jewish and Roman law, and having been found guilty by the former, is brought before Pilate who, finding no guilt in him, washes his hands of the whole matter.

The exact circumstances surrounding the death of Jesus are extremely obscure. The Gospels insist that he was crucified, but such a death is most improbable for it was distinctly against Roman law as crucifixion was not a punishment meted out to civil prisoners, being reserved for robbers and murderers. Even in the early centuries, the crucifixion was a mooted question, and we can sum up the early opinions in a few sentences:

According to the Gnostics of the first century, it was not Jesus but Simon the Cyrenean who died upon the cross in Jesus' place. Other early schools which held the divinity of Jesus as Christ declared that an illusion was sent by God upon the people so that they appeared to see him die, but that Christ as God could not die or even appear to die. Another school insists that he was taken from the cross, still alive and resuscitated, and that he left Syria, traveling eastward on a journey to India. These accounts accept the crucifixion as at least a partial reality, but Irenaeus, one of the early fathers contemporary with the Disciples and claiming to have spoken with some of them, declared that Jesus died in fullness of years. In the Jewish records, a prophet, who some have tried to identify as Jesus, was stoned to death by an incited mob. Be these opinions as they may, Jesus disappeared from history and tradition in his thirty-third year, completing in less than three years a Ministry that was to affect the whole of civilization, and from its humble beginnings in the barren, rocky lands of Syria was to spread to every corner of the earth.

THE TEACHINGS OF THE MASTER

The principal sources of information concerning the teachings of Jesus are, of course, the Gospels and Epistles to which may be added a few fragments from the Ante and Post Nicean fathers. The orthodox churches have rejected the Gnostic Gospels and such words of Jesus as were recorded in the Apocryphal texts. The teachings of Jesus in the Gospels are for the most part simple statements of spiritual or moral truths intended for the comparatively uneducated multitudes who gathered to hear his words. From the beginning, the church Was perplexed by the absence of a systematic religious or philosophical system. They coped with the problem in two ways: first by incorporating the Mosaic theology into the Christian system to give foundation and background to the sermons of the Master; second by a series of church councils they legislated into existence a Christianized system of philosophy which they distinguished by the term orthodox or canonical.

Actually, there is no evidence to prove that modern Christianity, particularly modern church organization, is really founded upon or consistent with the original teachings of Jesus. Rather, the church is the product of a dilemma, the result of numerous interpretations and reforms. The absence of facts always results in a chaos of opinions. There is no other religion in the world in which there are so many discordant sects, each claiming a peculiar integrity of interpretation. It is extremely difficult, after the passing of nineteen centuries, to discover with anything resembling certainty the genuine precepts of Christian, doctrine.

There are three principal schools of interpretation, founded upon three opinions as to the nature of Jesus himself. We may say that the first school assumes the humanity of Jesus, by this we mean that it regards him as a highly evolved, learned and unselfish man who as a man lived, preached and died a martyr to his ideals. This school consequently encourages the development of the moral virtues, fosters learning and has as its goal the ultimate elevation of all men to a similar state of perfection, with Jesus as their example and inspiration. The second school affirms that Jesus was of a divine and also human nature; human in his birth, growth and education, but divine in his ministry. The spirit of God descended upon him at the Baptism by John and from the Baptism to the Crucifixion, he was the very embodiment of God. The words of Jesus are therefore divine and infallible utterances. It is the duty of the pious Christian to accept without question not only the teachings of Jesus but the dogma of his divinely over-shadowed church. The third school denies the humanity of Christ, maintaining stoutly that Jesus was God and that the whole life was a divine mystery unique in the history of humanity, superior to every other spiritual tradition of the race. This school also places man in a negative position of a supplicant, being nothing in himself and depending entirely upon divine grace for his salvation.

It is evident that these are hopelessly irreconcilable premises, and it is also evident that sects built up around these premises would be in constant conflict with each other. In the end argument and confliction over-shadow the moral and ethical teachings so that principles are lost in a confusion of creeds.

It does not seem to have occurred to most theologians that Jesus was himself a mystic and spoke in the mystical sense, speaking of matters beyond the experience of many and beyond the understanding of most. Probably the most tragic misunderstanding that has come out of the misconceptions of interpreters is the orthodox conclusion already noted that Jesus was God incarnate and that by that very fact Christianity occupies an ineffable place among the beliefs of man. This mistake is due to a complete ignorance on the part of the average member of the Christian laity as to the meaning of the mystical theology of the ancient Mysteries. Jesus, speaking in terms of mystical realization, is interpreted literally by a misunderstanding world. Jesus, as an initiate of Oriental mysteries, says: "I and my Father are one" where upon the ignorant orthodox thinker interprets this to mean that God in proper person withdrew into the body of Jesus and functioned therefrom. The words of Jesus actually mean that he had discovered in himself his identity with universal truth and life. The mystic knows what Jesus the initiate meant when he said that he came "to bear witness," but the narrow-minded have attempted to make out of a great spiritual truth the material for a small creedal notion. The words of Jesus concerning his relationship with divinity are typical of the utterances of all illumined mystics, but only the illumined mystic can properly understand the language of the soul. The words of Jesus regarding his identity with God are truths in spirit, and to literalize them is to defame and destroy then significance.

Although Jesus preached in Judea and was first of all a prophet unto the Jews, it is a mistake to say that his teachings are primarily Judaic. Jewish elements are certainly present but so also are Egyptian and Grecian elements. With peculiar tolerance which evidences a generous understanding, he calls mankind to a high standard of integrity. He invites them to concern their minds with spiritual matters and admonishes them that they shall put the affairs of the spirit before those of the body. Jesus preached simplicity of living, honesty and virtue. He denounces a corrupted priestcraft for departing from the simple truths of the ancient patriarchs. As an ascetic he holds out the advantages of detachment from earthly interests, but in all his teachings he is practical and gentle.

The two most important sermons are the Sermon on the Mount and the Sermon delivered to the disciples on the occasion of the Last Supper. Together, these two Sermons are Christianity, yet how deliberately and intentionally the words of the Master have been misunderstood. In his parables he points out the morals of thrift and devotion, and to the world he gave his Commandments—the true creed of Christendom: "These two commandments I give unto you, that thou shalt love the Lord thy God with all thy heart and all thy soul, and thy neighbor, as thyself."

These two Commandments are the perfect summary of the whole Christian doctrine and Christian life. Jesus explicitly states that only those who perform these two Commandments with their whole heart shall have the right to call themselves his followers.

It seems then that in substance and fact there is no confusion in Christian doctrine, yet in the clash of creeds these two fundamental and inevitable principles of Christian living have been sacrificed and ignored and, in their place, have been advanced an elaborate and involved system which, with all its presumptions, has failed to practice these fundamental truths.

There is a popular belief that St. Paul was the first to preach a mystical Christian doctrine opposing the literalism of St. Peter. Certain it is that Paul recognized Christ as a spirit dwelling in man and not as a historical personality. This does not necessarily mean that Paul denied the existence of the historical Jesus or his Ministry, but rather that he recognized the mystical factor in the Spiritual life. In the Epistles Paul clearly, indicates that he is conversant with Eastern metaphysics and sees in Christianity a Mystery School teaching simple moral truths to the profane but reserving for the initiated a deeper and carefully concealed doctrine. In some respects, it is remarkable that the Paulian viewpoint was admitted into the Canonical texts, for even the superficial reader must realize that there are startling inconsistencies between the Gospels and Paul's letters. There is also considerable internal evidence that the writings of Paul were "doctored" to make the contradictions less glaring, so that the modern reader discovers to his astonishment that Paul appears to contradict himself. The truth of the matter is that Paul, who never met the Master in the flesh, alone perceived the spiritual significance of the Life and Ministry. The Apostles saw with their eyes and tried to record what they saw, accepting all things in the flesh, Paul saw with the spirit, perceiving inwardly and recording Christianity not as a sect or a doctrine but as a mystical experience.

The viewpoint of Paul is sustained by the Gnostic Gospels and the metaphysical tradition. Jesus, the initiate, stands out as a teacher of an esoteric tradition. It becomes evident that a true Christian is one "christened" within, not a follower after sects. Not by the Sacraments of the church but by the sanctification of the life is the righteous man admitted into the Assembly. Words without works are dead. True Christianity is not a faith but a discipline, not an acceptance but an achievement.

The early church, patterned after pagan Mysteries, sought for a little time to perpetuate the arcana, but such a procedure would doom the church to a humble and obscure existence, ministering only to a devout and dedicated few. The bishops of the church were mortal men instinctively desiring power and authority, and they sacrificed the spiritual doctrines of Christianity to temporal ambitions. The majority of mankind neither desires to improve itself nor to support an organization which demands a high degree of integrity. The outer body of the church increased to the degree that the standards of Christian living were lowered until at last, promising everything and demanding only temporal support, the church gained temporal power at the expense of spiritual authority. It is for this reason particularly that the

Christian thinker must never confuse the Jesus of Nazareth with the Christ of the modern church. Nor must the Christian thinker permit the clergy to interpret for him spiritual matters of which the clergy itself is ignorant.

The proof of what we say is the present state of Christendom which is evidently and undeniably woefully lacking in nearly all of the virtues which the Master taught. Jesus stated that those who claimed to be his followers should do his works, that it should live the truths which he taught. Yet Christian society is not founded upon Christian ethics. The Master said "love ye one another" but Christian nations do not love one another, Christian sects do not love one another, and the peoples of Christendom do not love one another. Glaring inconsistency is due to the pernicious teaching that theology, by a special dispensation, is empowered to save man in spite of what he is instead of because of what he is.

There is no great teacher whose doctrines have been more intentionally misunderstood than those of Jesus, but the intelligent thinker is able to distinguish clearly between Christianity and churchianity. Churchianity prays and pleads and exhorts, with formulas for every failing of the soul, washing out all the sins of man with holy water. The real teaching of Jesus simply states that he who lives the life shall know the doctrine.

QUOTATIONS FROM THE WORDS OF JESUS AS RECORDED BY ST. JOHN

"I am come a light into the world, that whosoever believeth on me should not abide in darkness."

"Verily, verily, I say unto you, the servant is not greater than his Lord; neither he that is sent greater than He that sendeth him."

"A new commandment I give unto you, that ye love one another; as I have loved you, that ye also love one another."

"In my Father's house are many mansions: if it were not so, I would have told you."

"Believest thou not that I am in the Father, and the Father in me? The words that l speak unto you I speak not of myself: but the Father that dwelleth in me, he doeth the works."

"If ye love me, keep my commandments."

"Greater love hath no man than this, that a man lay down his life for his friends."

"I came forth from the Father, and am come into the world: again, I leave the world and go to the Father."

"My doctrine is not mine, but his that sent me."

"Except a man be born again, he cannot see the kingdom of God."

"But the hour cometh, and now is, when the true worshippers shall worship the Father in spirit and in truth: for the Father seeketh such to worship him. God is a spirit: and they that worship him must worship him in spirit and in truth."

Yours sincerely,

Manly P. Hall

P. S. There is still time to order Mr. Hall's books for Christmas presents to yourself or your friends. All orders will be filled the day received. Mr. Hall will autograph any bound book upon request.

LOS ANGELES, CALIF., JAN. 1937

Dear Friend,

PADMA SAMBHAVA

Prior to the advent of Buddhism, Tibet was an inaccessible land peopled with savage and even cannibalistic tribes engaged in almost constant civil war. Occasionally, several of these clans would consolidate for the purpose of invading Chinese territory. The Tibetan religion was a species of Shamanism called Bon, consisting chiefly of ritualistic dances and offerings to appease the hosts of demons who were presumed to take continual offense at the actions of men. Previous to the coming of the Buddhist monks the tribes of Tibet possessed no history or written language, and their arts and crafts were aboriginal when compared with those of their Hindu and Chinese neighbors.

Until the end of the seventh century A.D. even Chinese were unable to penetrate Tibet. There is evidence, however, that at some very early time occult practices were introduced into the almost inaccessible Tibetan highlands and that temples of religious mysticism were built there prior to the Christian era. Such institutions produced little effect upon the general status of the people and little now remains as proof of their existence, other than highly magnified legends in Buddhist books dealing with the prehistoric periods. In one account, Buddhist priests entered Tibet in the fifth century before Christ; in another a monastery was built at Mt. Kailas B.C. 137; and a third tradition describes several sacred relics of the Buddhist faith which fell from heaven in the fourth century A.D.

Modern historians, though pitifully uninformed on matters of Lamaist tradition, are inclined to discredit the existence of any Buddhistic influence among the Tibetans prior to the seventh century of the present era, and no complete history exists prior to the eleventh century, from which time a well-organized if somewhat embellished history is available.

The first European to reach Lhasa, the Vatican of Buddhism in Tibet, was the Roman Catholic missionary Father O'Doric of Pordenone who reached this stronghold of Lamaism about A.D. 1330. About A.D. 600 Sron Tsan Gampo ascended the throne of the consolidated clans of Central Tibet to continue the work of general organization begun by his father who had extended his domains from the valley of Yar-lun. Being only about sixteen years of age, the youthful king was easily influenced by his two young and attractive wives, Bhrikuti, the daughter of the king of Nepal, and Wen-cheng, a Chinese princess. Both of these royal ladies were firm adherents of the Buddhist faith. When Sron Tsan Gampo sued for the hand of the princess of Nepal, he addressed the following words to her father Amsuvarman, "I, the king of barbarous Tibet, do not practice the ten virtues, but should you be pleased to bestow on me your daughter, and wish me to have the Law, I shall practice the ten virtues * * * Though I have not the arts * * * if you so desire * * * I shall build five thousand temples." In this manner was Buddhism introduced into Tibet.

Sron Tsan Gampo dispatched to India the wisest of his ministers, the illustrious Thonmi Sambhota who remained studying for several years with Buddhist monks. He later returned to Tibet bringing with him what has come to be called the Tibetan alphabet and several fundamental books of Buddhist scriptures. Although Sron Tsan Gampo was undoubtedly the greatest of the early kings of Tibet, he did little more for Buddhism than to establish a precedent upon which later priests and princes were to build the complicated structure of Lamaism. He was not a religious man and led a life of warfare both abroad with his armies and at home with his wives. His Nepalese princess was of a choleric disposition and kept his household in an uproar out of jealousy of his Chinese wife. Sron Tsan Gampo was canonized after death because he had opened the way for the civilizing of Tibet, and in the Lamist pantheon is regarded as an incarnation of the great Bodhisattva Avalohitesvara, known to the Chinese as Kwan-yin. His two wives were also canonized as female aspects or Sakti's of a divine power, becoming the white and the green Taras respectively.

The first image of Buddha to come into Tibet was brought as part of the dowry of the Nepalese princess.

During the reign of Sron Tsan Gampo, the following Buddhist priests entered Tibet: Kusara and Sankara Brahmana from India; Sila Manju from Nepal; Hwashang Maha-Ts'e from China; and Tabuta and Ganuta from Kashmir.

Padma Sambhava was born in the Province of Udyana, a district Northwest of what is now called Kashmir. The exact date of his birth is uncertain, but for practical purposes we may say that the miraculous event occurred in the opening years of the 8th century. "The Lotus-born One," as he is most generally known among the peoples of Northern Asia, carries several titles. By the Tibetans he is called Guru Rinpoche, or the Precious Guru, or more simply, he is referred to as Lopon which means Teacher.

Udyana, the state from which the Master came, has long been associated with stories of magic and sorcery. Referring to this Northern area, Marco Polo wrote, "They have an astonishing acquaintance with devilries and enchantment, insomuch as they can make their idols speak. They can also by their sorceries bring on changes of weather, and produce darkness, and do a number of things so extraordinary that no one without seeing them would believe them."

In the opening years of the 8th century, the blind king Indra bodhi was ruler over the great country Udyana. His reign was marked with singular misfortune. Famines afflicted his people. The king, to relieve their sufferings, emptied his treasuries, impoverishing the state. Chief among the misfortunes was the death of the king's only son, so that the land was filled with mourning, suffering and despair. In the time of their great emergency, the king and the people prayed to the gods for help and brought many offerings to the shrines and temples of Buddha. And so sincere and devout were these people and so deep was their distress that the voice of their prayer ascended through all the Lokas, or worlds, and was heard by the ever-listening ear of Amitabha. The ever-meditating lord, seated upon his lotus throne above the universe, was moved to compassion by the prayers of the people of Udyana, and he realized within himself that help should be sent unto them. And instantly, by the mystery of realization, a beam of light came forth out of Amitabha, and pouring through all the worlds, flowed as a red ray of celestial effulgency upon the earth. And the red ray came to rest at last in the center of a sacred lake in the midst of Udyana.

Indra bodhi, the king, perceived in a vision the omen of a great happening. A golden thunderbolt descended from the heavens and rested in his hand, a great light filled the whole world, and the blindness of his eyes was cured. After the vision had passed, the king realized that a miracle had indeed been wrought, for his sight was restored and word came to him that a rainbow of light had come down from the heavens and floated upon the lotus lake of Dhana kosha. This light extended not only through all the elements of matter but illumined also the superphysical world, rendering luminous and exalted the whole of nature.

The king deeply pious and fervently grateful for the divine intercession, entered into a boat and floated out upon the lake. Here he saw floating upon the water, a lotus flower of transcendental beauty, far lovelier than any natural flower. In the midst of this lotus, seated upon its petals, was a beautiful and luminous child, bearing in his hand the thunderbolt and emitting from his body an indescribable radiance. Although the exact date is unobtainable, the event described is reported to have occurred on the 10th day of the 7th month of the Tibetan calendar, and the child was 8 years of age.

According to the legend, king Indra bodhi fell on his knees in the boat, worshipping the glorious child. "Who art thou?" he cried, "who is thy father? and what is thy country?" And the child made answer, "Who my father was I know! I come in accordance with the prophecy of Sakya Muni who said, 'Twelve hundred years after me * * * a person more famed than myself will be born from a lotus, and be known as Padma Sambhava the Lotus-born, and he shall be the teacher of my esoteric Mantra-doctrine, and shall deliver all beings from misery!"

Many were the adventures and accomplishments of this divine child as he grew up under the patronage of King Indra bodhi. He associated himself early with magicians and sages until his reputation for learning spread throughout India. He attended the celebrated University of Nalanda, achieving extraordinary distinction for his knowledge of spells and enchantments. It was therefore with the greatest of satisfaction that he answered the call of the Tibetan nobles to bring the religion of Buddha over the great passes of the Himalayas to the remote villages of Inner Mongolia. Bearing in his hand the scepter of Indra, the Vedic god of the Winds, and robed in the garments of his Order, Padma Sambhava began his arduous journey, driving before him a number of oxen loaded with Buddhist scriptures.

Arriving in the North land, the magician-teacher began a series of combats with the demons and evil spirits that lurked in the fastnesses of the mountains and valleys. He overcame them all and received in each community the acclaim and veneration of the people. The Tibetan accounts of the victories of the Blessed Guru over all the forces of evil—the furies, the serpent-gods, the witches, and a fantastic of symbolical monsters—constitute a considerable literature. These stories exhibit to great advantage the saint's magical powers and profundity of knowledge.

During his stay in Tibet, where he arrived in A.D. 147, Padma Sambhava not only conquered the hierarchies of demons which preyed upon the people, but also apparently successfully subdued the various tribes and states, binding them to an allegiance to the Buddhist faith. He forgave, it is said, most of the infernal creatures such as ghosts and spirits and demons, and bound them also with his spells so that their power of evil was destroyed. He even preached the law of Buddha in the shadowland so that even the specters might find the path to enlightenment.

Having chosen twenty-five disciples to perpetuate his most secret and magical formulas, he finally prepared to depart from Tibet because other lands were in need of his instruction and presence. According to the Tibetan tradition, he remained in the Himalaya country for fifty years, but it is more probable that he made several journeys to Tibet over a period of years, visiting various countries enroute. He brought much of the literature and science of India to the Tibetan people and when his time finally came to depart from them, he gathered a considerable assemblage of the leaders of the countries and gave a lengthy address of advice and encouragement to the king, the priests, the nobles and the people. He also explained where he had hidden book and manuscripts and secret inscriptions in sacred caverns throughout the country. He also announced that his journey was to take him to the kingdom of Langkah by which some modern scholars infer that he went to Ceylon. Another group believe that his destination was the Island of Java. The places referred to in the Tibetan annals as the Island of the copper mountain.

After Padma Sambhava had finished his farewell address to the people, a rainbow came down from the sky and surrounded him. Four great beings appeared, and he entered into a celestial chariot and was carried away in the sky in a Southwesterly direction, followed by a procession of devas and heavenly musicians, and the air was full of flowers. For twenty-five days and nights, the multitude remained assembled, and it was said they were able to see the Blessed Gurus chariot moving like a shooting star through the sky, growing smaller and smaller until at last it disappeared over the Southern horizon.

The tradition goes on to say that the Guru's adventures continue even to the present day. Whenever a great king is in need of instruction, Padma Sambhava enters into him and lives for a certain time and then, his work finished, he passes on to another country. In substance, therefore, we can say that the Teacher's life was marked by uncertainties as to the dates of both birth and death. He is not generally included in lists of great Teachers, but he certainly belongs among those mysterious mortals whose strange lives and amazing deeds have influenced the whole course of human progress.

The Founder of Lāmāism, St. Padma-sambhava.

FUNDAMENTAL TENETS OF LAMAISM

The morals and ethics of Lamaism are derived principally from Hindu Buddhism, which has been treated in some detail in a previous lesson. In Tibet however, the simple and austere pragmatism of Gautama is justified and demonstrated by an elaborate and complicated system of metaphysical speculation. In some instances, Lamaism deviates widely from Indian Buddhism to the degree of actually denying the earlier agnostic traditions of Buddha. This is particularly noticeable in the attitude of Lamaism towards evil. Gautama denied the existence of evil, whereas a considerable part of Lamaist ceremonialism is devoted to propitiating and appeasing evil spirits. The godless philosophy of Gautama thus becomes the basis of a complicated pantheism, celebrating the persons and powers of over eighty thousand gods and demons. On the other hand, the groundwork of Lamaism is far more theologically scientific than that of ancient Buddhism in that it catalogs and orders practically every aspect of natural law, bringing all knowledge, sacred and profane, into one vast body of religious learning.

The numerous and often apparently grotesque aspects of Lamaism are suspended from a great and essentially sound framework of cosmogony and anthropology. These far northern mystics have evolved a theory of existence so amazingly ramified that it confounds and bewilders the best evolved systems of western thinking. Lamaism is a system of Asiatic kabbalism, probably deriving its authority from the pre-Buddhistic Brahmins. It speculates in all five of the accepted fields of philosophy and explores fields of natural learning where occidental thinkers fear to tread.

Clarified of its demonism and reduced to a more or less orderly tradition, the substance of Lamaist metaphysics is as follows: The foundation of Lamaist speculation is established upon the acceptance of an ever-existing but unconditioned state to which the term "The Absolute" may be properly applied. This primordial and unchanging suspension of Infinite Force, this unacting action, unaging time, unthinking thought, unknowing knowledge is the source and substance of the universe which maintains existence, and though uncreated, supports creation, in the Tibetan system this Absolute, this non-entity, is referred to as Adi-Buddha.

Prof. Rhys-Davids, one of the greatest western authorities on Buddhism, declares that this being ADI-BUDDHA, or the primordial Buddha whom he believes to signify Primordial Wisdom and Infinite Mind, was devised as a philosophic symbolic figure in the tenth century A.D. Those who are acquainted with the esoteric elements of Buddhism, however, affirm that this BEING was recognized by the first earliest masters of the Buddhistic philosophy, for Gautama Buddha himself says: "From the very beginning have I roused, brought to maturity, and fully developed the Bodhisattva."

In his valuable work the Buddhism of Tibet Austine Waddell declares that the theories regarding ADI-BUDDHA have been in existence since the first century. To the uninitiated ADI-BUDDHA is the primordial God, but to the wise the state or condition which is not God but is that by virtue of which both gods and men are established. From the eternal subjectivity of ADI-BUDDHA manifests the first and most abstract objectification.

This manifestation is the LOGOS, thought, son of the Eternal Thinker. Being, progeny of not-being. Thing, issuing from no-thing. Numbers suspended from Number. ADI-BUDDHA causes to shine out from itself a single ray of absolute force and this ray is called VAJRADHARA, the Logos already referred to. VAJRADHARA, the first of the existing Buddhas, or, in the esoteric system of Lamaism, the first of intellects; for in this system of philosophy all creations and all creatures are modes of intelligence descending in a concatenated line from ADI-BUDDHA who's very being is the substance of Nirvana. VAJRADHARA, the eldest of all BEINGS out of NOT-BEING, is pictured as seated meditating in the midst of space, his immense being faintly shadowed midst the eternal sea of the Infinite.

VAJRADHARA is the eternal Meditator, the being in whom all things are epitomized, the mind in whom all minds are centered—existent but not creative. He can be defined in the words of Simon Magus, the Gnostic, who said of the first Logos that He "stood, stands and will stand."

It is not given to VAJRADHARA, however, to take the three great strides or steps by which the dimensions of space and the worlds that dwell therein are established. Therefore, from VAJRADHARA there issues forth the DIAMOND HEART—VAJRASATTVA—the second Logos. The Builder who creates all things by contemplation.

VAJRASATTVA emanates from itself the Seven Gods, the Architects of the universe, which in the Tibetan system are the DHYANA'S or Sons of Meditation. Literally, those who are created by the exercising of the contemplative power. In discussing the DHYANA BUDDHAS most writers refer to only five because the sixth and seventh belong wholly to the esoteric tradition as we shall presently observe. The five exoteric Dhyana Buddhas are the source, cause and substance of the five elements of the material world, of the five organs of power and the five faculties of sensation.

The Dhyana Buddhas, the Sons of Meditation, called the Parentless or the primeval Monads from the worlds of incorporeal things, may well be regarded as the vortices, or LAYA CENTERS, or vital points upon which the intellectual sphere is elevated. Are these not also the glorious blossoms referred to by Proclus which, descending from the divine nature, become the seven directions of the world, as in the Sepher Yetzirah, and the seven chakras or whirling wheels upon which the constitution of man is supported?

The next point to be carefully noted is that the Dhyana Buddhas are not terrestrial creatures, but beings established in the substance of intellect. In Platonic terms, they are the Ideas of the Seven Perfections, of which two must remain concealed. The names of the five known Dhyana's, together with the symbols with which they are associated by the Tibetans are as follows:

The first DHYANA BUDDHA is VAIROCHANA. The mutra, or hand posture, is that of the DHARMA CHAKRA, or the turning of the Wheel of the Law. He is seated upon a throne supported by a lion. His color is white, his element ether, and his symbol or insignia is the wheel with eight spokes. Because of his posture being that of the teaching, or turning of the wheel, he is regarded as the intellectual embodiment of the highest wisdom. In the Tantric banners, he is placed in the center and considered as the chief of the DHYANA'S.

The second DHYANA BUDDHA is AKSHOBHYA, whose hand posture is that of the earth touching, or the witness, for Buddha laid his right hand with the palm inward on his leg, pointing towards the ground to invoke the earth as a witness for his integrity at the time of the temptation by Mara. This is signified in the BHUSPARSA. This Dhyana Buddha is seated upon a throne supported by an elephant. His color is blue, his element air, and his peculiar symbol is the VAJRA, or thunderbolt. He is seated in the East.

The third DHYANA BUDDHA is RATNA, whose hand posture is called VARA, or the best bestowing. It is the posture of charity, with the palm turned upward away from the body. The Buddha is enthroned upon the back °f a horse. His color is gold and yellow, his element earth, and his symbol the RATNA or jewel. He is seated in the south.

The fourth DHYANA BUDDHA is AMITABHA, the Buddha of boundless love. His hand posture is that of DHYANA or meditation. The palms of the hands rest over each other in the lap. Sometimes a sacred vessel rests in the palms. The throne of AMITABHA is supported by the peacock, his color red, and his element fire. His symbol is the RAKTA PADMA, the red lotus, and he rules over the West, where his heaven is located.

The fifth, and last, of the DHYANA BUDDHAS is AMOGHASLDDHA, whose hand posture is that of the blessings of fearlessness, in which the right hand is held upward before the body, with the palm to the front. This DHYANA is seated on a winged dwarf, or unidentified creature called Shang-Shang. His color is green, his element water, and his symbol is the VISVA VAJRA, or crossed thunderbolt. He holds dominion over the northern corner of the world.

Thus are the five powers established, and in many Oriental countries figures of these DHYANA'S, or their reflections in the lower worlds, appear incorporated into their prolific religious art. "These Dhyani-Buddhas," writes H. P. Blavatsky, "emanate or create from themselves by virtue of Dhyana, celestial selves, the supermen Bodhisattvas. These incarnate at the beginning of every human cycle on earth as mortal men, becoming occasionally, owing to their personal merit, Bodhisattvas among the sons of humanity, after which they may reappear as MANUSHI (human) Buddhas. The ANUPA AKA (or Dhyani-Buddhas) are thus identical with the Brahmanical MANA SAPUTRA, the 'mind-born' sons."

According to the teaching of Lamaism the Dhyani-Buddhas are reflected downward through four worlds to become in the lowest, heroic personalities. Thus, the attributes of God in the first world become hierarchies in the second, sidereal bodies in the third, and divine men in the fourth. The divine impulses, striking the various levels of manifestation, evolve vehicles upon these levels. In the constitution of man, the ideas, or principles, of the Dhyana's may become sense perceptions; or in the world they may become races, in the constitution of the earth continents, in the solar system planets, and in the cosmos those abstract or divine substances which in the lower world manifest as the elemental essences. As these Dhyana's come into concrete manifestation, their correspondences appear within the sphere of our perceptions, for the sixth Dhyana will bring with him the sixth continent, the sixth race, the sixth round, the sixth sense, the sixth element, etc.

Through their shadows, or manifestations, these Dhyana's are also the directors of the great world periods, or "ages." and all such divisions existing in it. They are also concerned with the substances of one of these five meditating divinities. It has already been intimated that each of the Dhyani Buddhas caused to issue out of itself a Bodhisattva, or spiritual entity, which is an aspect of itself. These Bodhisattvas are collective objectifications of the subjective Dhyani's. In the active labor of creation these Dhyana's, in order to accomplish the molding of the several orders of life, project shapes or personalities which they overshadow. These overshadowed entities exist on several planes simultaneously, and through them the forces of the Dhyana's are manifested.

Thus, in one sense of the word, the first root race upon the earth was a VEHAN (vehicle) for the first Dhyana Buddha. Therefore, the root race as a whole might be regarded as a Bodhisattva, or body, for the expression of the wisdom of the Diamond Heart. Because it was established in wisdom and by wisdom, the first race could not perish from the earth. At the end of the first race, VAIROCHANA incarnated as SAMANTABHADRA, and was released in the form of the first MANUSHI or human Buddha, KRA-KU-CANDRA.

The second Dhyana Buddha, Akshobhya's, at the end of the second root race, incarnated a Vajrapani, and was released as the human Buddha—KANAKA MUNI.

The third Dhyana Buddha, Ratna, at the end of the third root race incarnated as RATNAPANI, and was released as the human Buddha, KASYAPA.

The fourth Dhyana Buddha, Amitabha, at the end of the fourth root race, incarnated as Avalokitesvara, and was released as the human Buddha, GAUTAMA.

The fifth Dhyana Buddha, Amogasiddha, will incarnate at the end of the fifth root race as Visva ani, and will be released as the human Buddha—MAITREYA.

When we consider the background of Gautama in this system, we find his descent from ADI BUDDHA through Vajra Dhara and Vajra Dhara as follows: He is from the Dhyana Amitabha, the lord of enlightened love, whose western paradise is open to all who have achieved to virtue and integrity. His Bodhisattva aspect is Avalokitesvara, from which has been derived the Kwannon concept of mercy, for Avalokitesvara is the origin of the Japanese Kwannon and the Chinese Kwan-yin. The Dalai Lama of Tibet presumes to be the incarnation of Avalokitesvara, which reminds the careful student that the Bodhisattva aspect did not cease when Gautama became perfected as the Buddha. This is because Gautama simply represents the personality in whom the Bodhi sattvic forces were perfected. These forces are universal and will remain throughout the Kalpa.

We find the universe upheld by the warp and woof of the divine names, even as the Tibetan world is upraised upon the crossed thunderbolts of Indra. These divine names are but another way of identifying the states or conditions which in the, Buddhistic system are Dhyana's and Bodhisattvas. Zen, the highest form of Buddhistic tradition, assures us that all this concatenation of divinities but symbolizes modes of mind moving through the diversity of the phenomenal sphere. Whenever we assume a mode of mind, that mode becomes incarnate in us. The universe is upheld by five major modes which, manifesting through the planes, produce an infinitude of complex effects. It would probably be more correct to say that there are seven modes of intellect, for the two invisible and unknown are also actually in manifestation, although we do not respond to their impulses consciously at the present time.

The Dhyani Buddhas are collective ideas manifesting through their Bodhisattvas—collective thoughts or minds—which, in turn, are revealed in physical life collectively through the racial brain and individually through highly evolved types, of which the highest in each case becomes the Manushi Buddha, or the human vehicle through which the law is released into expression. The order is, therefore, first an idea, then a mind to contain it. As Idea manifests through mind, so mind, in turn becomes temporarily represented through brain. Thus, Gautama is the brain of Avalokitesvara even as Amitabha is the Idea. It would be a mistake, however, to consider that Amitabha, the boundless Idea, should have no manifestation other than Gautama. Everything passing through the fifth of its seven states is manifesting the Avalokitesvara forces and is under the control of that ray.

An understanding of the metaphysical elements of Buddhism can only result from a knowledge of the Brahminic framework of the system. We can summarize it in this way.

From that which is eternal—Atma—issued Buddhi, the Link, and Manas, the Diamond Heart. From Manas, or Mind, come forth the seven Meditations, or thoughts, of which five have come to be known and two remain concealed. Upon these Thoughts, all creation is established and the reactions or reciprocal relations of these Thoughts produce the complexes and reflexes of life. In every case, the pure thought, or meditation, comes to the rescue of the confused condition. The heterogeneity arising from the blending of divergent modes is clarified by the periodic appearance in each of the seven ages of the pure thought of that age; which thought, embodied in a perfected mortal, releases the age from bondage to confusion and error.

When the Seven Thoughts of the Eternal Thinker have been released to their primitive state of suspension above action, by meditation, then the Diamond Heart will cease to feel or know the seven Dhyana's or modes of intellect. Instantly these will cease and the Heart itself will retire into the eternal meditating Buddha, who in turn will be absorbed into the Absolute state, Nothing is real but Adibuddha, and all existence consists of conditions arising from the various forces of ignorance of this fact. The Buddhas are established to correct through their teachings and lives those forms of ignorance which cause man to forget that the universe is composed simply of thoughts and dependent for existence upon the directionalization of the wills of the seven Dhyani's whose meditations, reflected into every atom of space, establish the inevitability of the septenary law in Nature.

EXTRACTS FROM TIBETAN PHILOSOPHY.

Whatever is unpleasing to yourself do not to another.

Whatever happiness is in the world has all arisen from a wish for the welfare of others. Whatever misery there is has arisen from indulging selfishness.

There is no eye like the understanding, no blindness like ignorance, no enemy like sickness, nothing so dreaded as death.

A king is honored in his own dominions, but a talented man everywhere.

THE FOUR PRECIPICES IN SPEECH.

If speech be too long, it is tedious; if too short, its meaning is not appreciated; if rough, it ruffles the temper of the hearers; if soft, it is unsatisfying.

THE EIGHT ACTS OF LOW-BORN PERSONS.

Using coarse language, impoliteness, talking with pride, want of foresight, harsh manners, staring, immoral conduct, and stealing.

THE TEN FAULTS.

Unbelief in books, disrespect for teachers, rendering one's self unpleasant, covetousness, speaking too much, ridiculing another's misfortune, using abusive language, being angry with old men or with women, borrowing what cannot be repaid, and stealing.

Yours sincerely, MANLY P. HALL

FEB. 15, 1937

Dear Friend,

AKHNATON, ADORER OF THE ATON.

Amen-hotep IV, the Golden Hawk, King of Upper and Lower Egypt, the Only One of Ra, Son of the Sun, Great in Duration, the Mighty Bull, Lofty of Plumes, Beloved of Amon-Ra, and Lord of Heaven, was born at Thebes in the year B.C. 1388 (?). The name Amen-hotep, in Greek Amenophis, means "the peace of Amon." This great king was the only surviving son of Amen-hotep III and his consort Queen Tiy. On his father's side, he was descended from Thutmosis III, the Spoiler of his Enemies, the conqueror of Syria, and the Smiter of the Princes of Zahi. It was Thutmosis III who built up the Empire which fell in the reign of Amen-hotep IV. Queen Tiy, a woman of extra-ordinary abilities, for many years Regent of the Double Empire, is said to have been of Syrian origin. In the opinion of Dr. E. Wallis Budge, it was the alien blood of his mother and grandmother that was responsible, in part at least, for the multitude of strange ideas on religion, government and art that dominated the mind of Amen-hotep IV.

The childhood of the young Pharaoh seems to have been a continual struggle against the limitations of health which afflicted so many of his dynasty. Amen-hotep III, surnamed the Magnificent, appears to have been an incurable invalid, who had been married to the Princess Tiy in his twelfth year. It was the tendency of the entire family to marry at an extremely early age.

When Amen-hotep IV had reached his twelfth year, his health brought general concern not only to his family but to the whole Empire. If he died childless, the dynasty would end. A suitable bride was therefore sought among the vassal states, and a hasty marriage was contracted. Royal families did not seem to enjoy good health in those days. Marriageable daughters of noble birth were difficult to find, many dying in childhood. The prince was united in marriage with an Egyptian girl named Nefertiti, she was of noble birth, the daughter of a Prince named Ay. At the time of this marriage, the Pharaoh was about twelve years of age and his bride was nine or ten. A short time after the marriage, Amen-hotep III died in his early fifties, leaving the crown to the thirteen-year-old invalid who already showed a strange tendency to visions and dreams.

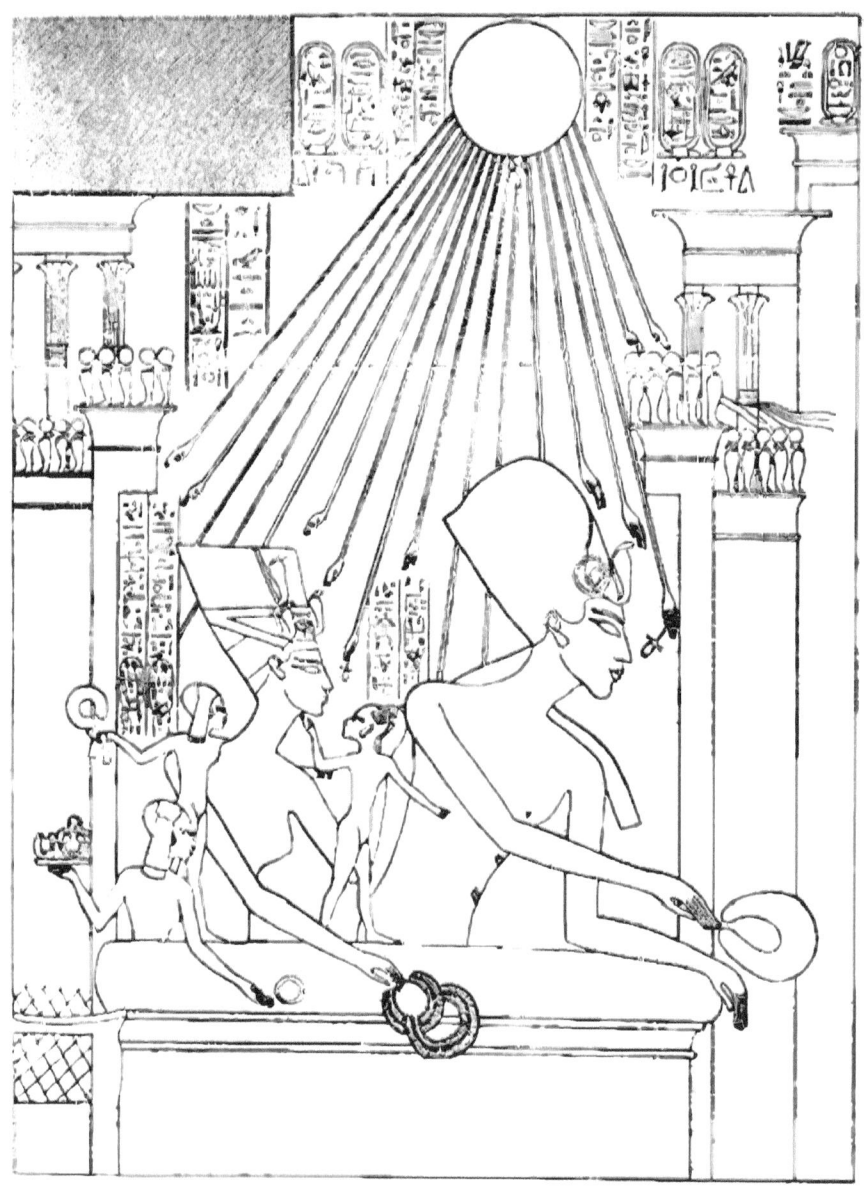

AKHNATON WITH HIS QUEEN AND THREE OF THEIR DAUGHTERS ON THE BALCONY OF HIS PALACE. AKHNATON IS BESTOWING GIFTS, AND IN THE SKY ABOVE IS THE RADIANT ATON, ITS RAYS ENDING IN HUMAN HANDS.

In addition to being the Wearer of Diadems, Amen-hotep IV was High Priest of Ra-Horakhti, Sovereign of the spirits, souls and bodies of the Egyptian people—Priest-King of the greatest Empire on earth. There is a legend to the effect that Queen Tiy, longing for a son, had vowed him to the gods before his birth. Be this true or not, from earliest childhood, the young Pharaoh was more of a priest than a statesman and well deserved the title "the Great of Visions." Arthur Weigall thus describes the young King: One may imagine now the Pharaoh as a pale, sickly youth. His head seemed too large for his body; his eyelids were heavy, his eyes were eloquent of dreams. His features were delicately molded, and his mouth, in spite of a somewhat protruding lower jaw, is reminiscent of the best of the art of Rosetti. He seems to have been a quiet, studious boy, whose thoughts wandered in fair places, searching for that happiness which his physical condition had denied to him. His nature was gentle; his young heart overflowed with love. He delighted, it would seem, to walk in the gardens of the palace, to hear the birds singing, to watch the fish in the lake, to smell the flowers, to follow butterflies, to warm his small bones in the sunshine. Already he was sometimes called "Lord of the breath of sweetness!"

Amen-hotep IV ruled Egypt for seventeen years. During the first four years of his reign, he exercised little individual authority. Queen Tiy, as Regent, was the actual Sovereign. She was deeply impressed by the extraordinary mentality of her son and recognized in him forces more divine than human. The young King matured early, and by his seventeenth or eighteenth year was the actual governor of his country.

The inevitable conflict between the youthful idealist and the priesthood of Amon-Ra took definite shape in the fifth and sixth years of his reign. Most writers, in comparing the religious ideals of Amen-hotep IV with those of Amon-ism, speak in most depreciatory terms of Egypt's state religion. There is no doubt that the conquests of Thutmosis III and the magnificence of Amen-hotep III had filled the temples with priceless treasures. It is also quite possible that grandeur had deflected the priests from their sacred duties and had allowed innumerable corruptions to undermine the integrity of their cult. This was not entirely the fault of the priests, however, for in Egypt the Pharaoh was both priest and king, and a ruler given to war and plunder, being likewise the chief priest of the state religion, set a bad example to the whole priesthood. We may therefore say that the religions of Egypt were corrupted from the top down. When spirituality failed in the prince, it disappeared from the temples.

It would be quite wrong to deny a deep spiritual significance to the ancient Egyptian religion. The gods of the various names, or provinces, of the Empire were symbols of the great spiritual truths of life. The Mysteries of Egypt were among the deepest of religious institutions, and the secret doctrines of India and the old world were preserved in the adyta of the Egyptian temples.

In examining the religious beliefs of Amen-hotep IV, we should not therefore think of his religion as entirely original. Rather, he had perceived certain corruptions and limitations in the state religion, and, being a man of exceptional spiritual perception, he attempted to correct these errors by a new interpretation of the spiritual facts of life. It is difficult to say now whether he actually founded Aton-ism, or merely encouraged a religious tendency already arising among his people. Certainly, he did not invent the term Aton, but rather gave new profundity to symbols and beliefs that had descended from the remote periods of Egyptian beginnings. The King's philosophy did not develop immediately into its final state but evolved gradually over a period of several years. It is quite probable that during this period of unfoldment the King had the assistance and advice of religious reformers and philosophers who helped him to shape the general structure and define the boundaries of his reformation. He drew away from the state religion, gradually breaking one after another the immemorial traditions of the Empire.

It was when Amen-hotep IV reached the nineteenth year of his life that he broke finally with the priesthood of Amon-Ra. He did not immediately attempt the overthrow of the Theban hierarchy.

Rather, he set up his own faith in the midst of his adversaries, giving it the influence and authority of his own position as demi-god of the Nile. It was after this official break with the old hierarchy that he changed his name. Amen-hotep is a name rooted in the faith of Amon; therefore, it was no longer appropriate for a ruler who had withdrawn his allegiance to the old order. The name which he chose, and by which he is now remembered, was Akhnaton, which means "the Aton is satisfied."

Having broken forever with the old faith, Akhnaton found the way before him far from easy. The city of his fathers was dedicated to the elder gods. The state religion was firmly ensconced in the hearts and lives of the people. As time passed, he realized that he must not only break with the ancient faith, but he must also depart from its city and all of the ties of tradition and culture that flourished there. The young Pharaoh chose a site for his new capital about a hundred and sixty miles up the Nile from Cairo. Here he built the city of Khut-en-Aton—the Horizon of Aton. When he came to the site, he spoke to all who were assembled there, and they bowed before his will, and did homage to him, and these are his words: "Ye behold the city of the Horizon of Aton, which the Aton has desired me to make for Him as a monument, in the great name of my Majesty forever. For it was Aton, my Father, that brought me to this City of the Horizon."

His new city, with its temple to the Formless One being at last inhabitable, Akhnaton took up his residence there in the eighth year of his reign. Accompanied by his nobles, bearing the records of the Empire, and followed by a considerable concourse of people, Akhnaton went forth to officially dedicate his new capital. With his queen and their three children, the young King established himself in a palace ornamented with carvings which represented the symbols of his faith. It was in the freer and more refined atmosphere of Khut-en-Aton that the Pharaoh actually established his religion. The spiritual ministry of Akhnaton commenced in his twenty-second year. Here, in the shadow of great stone temples, was born the doctrine of the True Aton, the Universal God, a doctrine of such profundity that it has moved scholars to say that Akhnaton was the first enlightened man of recorded history.

Charles F. Potter, in his history of religion, writes: "He (Akhnaton) was also the first pacifist, the first realist, the first monotheist, the first democrat, the first heretic, the first humanitarian, the first internationalist, and the first person known to attempt to found a religion. He was born out of due time, several thousand years too soon."

Abounding in virtues unusual to his time, inspired by motives incomprehensible to his contemporaries, Akhnaton suffered as all idealists must suffer. From the eighth to thirteenth years of his reign, Akhnaton seems to have been principally concerned with the perfection of his doctrine in the city which he had built. Budge describes him as living a strange life of religious and artistic propaganda. The Empire flourished under his benevolent direction. Also, during this period, his mother died, and his fourth daughter was born. Tiy, the Queen Mother, seems to have exercised a powerful influence over her son's political attitudes. She was a modifying and restraining force, and very possibly remained to her death in the faith of Amon. His respect for his mother held Akhnaton's religious enthusiasm within certain bounds, but with her passing, this restraint was removed.

By his twenty-fifth and twenty-sixth years, Akhnaton must have realized he had not much longer to live in this world. His constitution always delicate, was growing constantly weather under the strain of his over-active mind. The Pharaoh therefore changed his program. He was no longer content with his own city dedicated to the True God. He began a powerful campaign to spread his religion among the cities and provinces of his Empire. In the early period of his religion, he described God as "the Heat which is in the Aton." His unfolding consciousness brought a fuller realization, and he gave a new definition: "the Effulgency which comes from the Aton." The change indicates definitely a deepening spiritual understanding, and an increasing grasp of the mystical factors of a great theology.

Soon after the death of Queen Tiy, Akhnaton issued an edict that the name of Amon should be erased from every inscription in Egypt. So complete and thorough was the work of his agents, that scarcely a statuette remained in which the hated name was not defaced. Even the tomb of Queen Tiy was broken into and the cartouches upon her mummy-case destroyed. The names of kings which included some form of the word Amon were obliterated, and all who carried a name embodying the hated word were forced by law to assume some other title. This extreme action could only have resulted from extreme persecution and from the Pharaoh's realization that only by the most drastic steps could his reformation be accomplished before his own life ended.

Akhnaton was about twenty-six years old when his fifth daughter was born. True to the traditions of the dynasty, Akhnaton desired a son to carry on his work, but in the fourteenth year of his reign a sixth daughter was born, and the following year a seventh daughter completed his family, and thus the Pharaoh died without a male heir. Much has been made of Akhnaton's domesticity. Certainly, no other Pharaoh is so often depicted m the informal domestic relationships. In carvings, Akhnaton is frequently shown with his arm about his beautiful wife Nefertiti, a pose entirely strange to Egyptian art. The couple are often shown surrounded by their children, or playing with them. In the fifteenth year of his reign, Akhnaton began the construction of his tomb, but the work was never finished, and his body was finally placed in the vault of his mother, where it was discovered in 1907.

The last two years of Akhnaton's reign may be regarded as the period of discouragement. The faith he had founded was not strong enough to withstand the ever-present priesthood of Amon. Only a few of the most intelligent Egyptians could understand what he was trying to teach. The world was not ready for the rule of love. Added to his other perplexities were the clouds of war. It was the Hittite invasion of Syria that prepared the way for the end. Conspirators arose, the vassal countries that looked to Egypt for protection sent messengers in vain. The governors of provinces pled for help against the invaders and traitors, but Akhnaton would not send arms. To the dreamer king, Aton was the One Father of all men and this ever-living God would not sanction war and pillage. The Pharaoh stood firm, but his firmness was of no avail. His cities were conquered. Little by little, his revenues ceased, for his governors no longer had provinces to tax. In two short years, the magnificent Empire of Thutmosis III was bankrupt.

The strain of these troublous times destroyed what little health remained to the Pharaoh. With the collapse of his Empire, Akhnaton died. His end appears to have been sudden, for modern scientists who have examined the mummy are of the opinion that the end was due to a stroke. The body was no longer able to bear the worry and sorrow of a broken heart.

On the front of his coffin, he is called "Akhnaton, the Beautiful Child of the living Aton, whose name shall live forever and ever." How strangely sad, how strangely beautiful, is the prayer to the One Universal Father which was found inscribed on golden foil beneath the feet of the mummified body of Akhnaton: "I breathe the sweet breath which comes forth from Thy mouth. I behold Thy beauty every day. It is my desire that I may hear Thy sweet voice, even the North wind, that my limbs may be rejuvenated with life through love of Thee. Give me Thy hands, holding Thy spirit, that l may receive it and may be lifted by it. Call Thou upon my name unto eternity, and it shall never fail."

Thus, passed from this life a soul too fragile to bear the shocks of flesh. With Akhnaton passed also the faith he had founded, the city he had built, and the dream of peace which had filled his heart. Great Amon reigned again, supreme and plumed with power. More than three thousand years have passed since Akhnaton wrestled with the gods of Egypt. The homage of the modern world, a little wiser in the mysteries of spirit, may be best expressed in the words of Professor Breasted: "There died with him such a spirit as the world had never seen before."

Another modern student of the philosophy of Akhnaton, Mrs. Julia Ellsworth Ford, concisely states the great Pharaoh's position in the evolution of civilization in her interesting article Akhnaton: PHARAOH AND PROPHET:

"Akhnaton thus emerges as one of the most remarkable characters that have ever been born into the world. He was a prophet, a teacher of truth and sincerity, a seer, a philosopher, a reformer, a great poet, an architect, a lover of music. He was a brave and fearless rejector of dogma, tradition, superstition,—it is amazing the way he threw them off like dead leaves to the wind. Although a king, he believed in democracy and made friends with people of peasant origin. In all history and romance, there is no man who loved a woman more devotedly than Akhnaton loved Nefertiti. His position as rider, his religion, his honors—all he shared equally with her—"my great wife, Nefertiti," as he called her. For the first time in history, three thousand years ago, a government was run on the principle of Love. It was not his principles, but the lack of principle in his enemies that destroyed him."

THE RELIGIOUS TEACHING OF AKHNATON

The second millennium B. C. there was a period of extreme religious obscuration. The ancient world had not recovered from the collapse of the Atlantean culture. The great social institutions of prehistoric times no longer guided the course of empire. Humanity was adjusting itself to a new vision and new codes of living. The Mystery Schools still flourished but the number of adepts was small and the Secret Doctrine could only be given to people in fables, symbols and moral teachings of a simple nature. Most of the nations had their own gods, and an entirely national or tribal outlook on religious matters. The gods of Egypt were the guardians of the Egyptians, but had no place in their hearts for other races. India still paid homage to its ancient tribal deities, worships ping spirits of fire and air. The Jew propitiated his own peculiar god as the Lord of Israel and protector of his tribe. The Golden Age of philosophy had not come to Greece, and it was to be more than seven hundred years before Buddha was to release India from the misinterpretations of the Brahmins, and Pythagoras was to lift the Greeks to a first place among philosophic nations.

It was against the concept of a tribal god that Akhnaton hurled the strength of his inner conviction. He stood in the midst of images and altars raised to patron deities and tribal tutelary's. This enlightened Pharaoh raised his voice in a glorious hymn of praise to the one secret and eternal Spirit that ruled all men. To him, there were no longer gods of Karnak, gods of Luxor, gods of Thebes. To him, there was no longer Jehovah, Adonis or Amon-Ra. There was one God, and, though His names were many, His essence was indivisible.

Picture a twenty-year-old boy, born to luxury and power, limited by the frailty of his body and the overwhelming strength of the tradition in which he lived. Perceiving clearly and surely a spiritual truth that was to change the whole life of the world, imagine the courage that it took to stand out against the gods of his fathers and to defy the priestcrafts that had ruled unquestioned for ages. The world has produced no braver spirit than Akhnaton, the Beautiful Child of Aton.

As High Priest of Ra-Horakhti, Akhnaton had often gazed into the face of the Sun-God. It was from meditating upon the cosmic significance of the sun that the young mystic came suddenly to understand the true meanings of light and good and truth. The Pharaoh realized that the sun did not shine only upon Egypt, nor did its light and heat protect only the cities where it was honored. Its rays shone beyond the mountains and beyond the deserts. Its light cheered the barbarians and sustained even the enemies of Egypt. Nor did it minister only to human beings. Under its benevolent rays, all nature flourished. Flowers opened to its light, many colored insects fluttered in its beams, and all the world was gladdened and rendered fertile by the luminous love of the solar orb.

It came forcibly to Akhnaton's mind that the sun symbolized not only the glory of God and the magnificence of the celestial power, but also the infinite tenderness and intimacy of life. The deity did not rule from a chariot in the heavens but flowed into all the earth, nursing tiny shoots in the ground, and painting flowers with numerous resplendent hues. It was a far cry from the great stone faces gazing down in aloofness from the shadows of the temples to the God of Akhnaton whose ever-present life gave strength to the wing of the bird and patient industry to the little creatures of the earth. Akhnaton found the spirit that dwells in the innermost and rules the furthermost. He bowed in adoration before the truth he had discovered and offered himself as a living sacrifice to the ever-living, ever-flowing sun.

As a symbol for his religion, Akhnaton chose the shining face of Aton—the solar disc. The effulgency of the Aton he represented by rays flowing in all directions from the solar face. Each of the rays ended in a human hand, to represent the active power of the light; and in some cases, these hands held the crux ansata, the symbol of the giving of life. The whole figure represented the hand of God in all things. "Give me Thy hands!" cried Akhnaton in his religious ecstasy. The young mystic walked with God, hand in hand with the ever-living light. Having realized inwardly that God was life and love and light, Akhnaton could find no place in the universe for ignorance and hate and evil.

It is the opinion of some Egyptologists that Akhnaton was the first human being who realized the Fatherhood of God and Brotherhood of Man. When he refused to send armies against the Hittites, he made the supreme sacrifice of his Empire and his life, fully convinced that a God of love desired that men should live together in peace. In his heart was the peace of the Aton, the spiritual sun. As Pharaoh of Egypt, he was the personification of the Aton, the high priest of Universal Truth. It was therefore his duty to perform the works of the Aton and to be a manifestation before men of the virtues resplendent in the sun. This seems to be the root of the Messianic doctrine. Akhnaton chose to bear witness, to conte as one crying in the wilderness—"prepare the way of the Lord, and make His paths straight."

Akhnaton therefore made another great discovery. He discovered the secret of the living of the Aton. Recognizing the presence of the Universal Father in himself, he strove to live as the personification of the light. His own heart was the brilliant face of the sun. His every thought and action must give life, like the innumerable hands which he figured on the rays of the Aton. In this way, Akhnaton achieved the mystical at-one-ment. He not only recognized the truth, but he applied it, making himself personally responsible for his part in the shining of the Aton.

There is a very subtle aspect to Akhnaton's philosophy of God. Amon-Ra was a heavenly king whose will all men must obey. Egypt bowed before the law which descended from heavenly rulers seated upon their great thrones in space. Akhnaton rejected the divine despotism. He did not bend to the dictates of the super-mundane Pharaohs. The laws of Aton flowed through the king. He lived in them and they in him. Not obedience, but understanding was his creed, for we fear what we obey, but we love what we understand. Akhnaton lifted up his heart in love to Aton and found at-one-ment with that universal love which enfolds all things in its mighty presence. In the dim past Akhnaton stands, enfolded in the Aton, luminous with the ageless light, lifted by his understanding into the very presence of the Ever-Shining One.

Akhnaton was too great for his own day, and, although thirty-three hundred years have passed, he is too great even for this modern world. Even Christianity has not accomplished the fulfillment of Akhnaton's dream. The tribal God survives, and in the twentieth century is still the jealous Father of the world. Only a few mystics have pierced the veil and found the Real. Jew and Gentile, Mohammedan and Brahmin, have not yet found the common denominator, and millions of earnest Christians worship a God of whims and tyrannies, a petty despot in the heavens. How many centuries yet must pass before men can discover the God of peace who loves all His children, and how many centuries must pass before His children will have the wisdom and courage to sacrifice life, wealth and power to the spirit of love that pervades every atom of the world?

It is impossible in the meager records that survive to outline the complete system of Aton-ism. The priests of Amon-Ra, when their power was regained, obliterated the records of the heretic King. For centuries the name of Aton was not spoken, the temple of the Disc of the Sun, with its rays and hands, fell to ruin, to be finally covered by the shifting sands of the desert. But this we do know—he was opposed to elaborate ceremonial and all the complicated machinery of the priestcraft. He worshipped Aton at its rising, the visible sun emerging from the night, the fulfillment of the eternal promise. He worshipped Aton at its setting, the symbol of light descending into the dark earth, even as Aton, descending into the darkness of all things, hides its rays in nature, to shine forth only as the works of nature, Aton, hidden with good words, good thoughts, and good deeds, is the ever-flowing proof of the hidden Reality. Akhnaton offered prayers to the Aton, prayers that were the symbol of his own integrity yearning for the Real. In his great mystical joy, the King had to sing, and his very song was a ray of light, the light of the Aton singing to the Aton. He made a simple offering also of fruit and flowers, and on rare occasions conformed in general to the spirit of Egyptian religion. But always he was honoring an ever-present Spirit, the absence of which was unthinkable. It was never necessary to invoke the ever-present, for the Aton, though without ears, heard all things; without eyes, saw all things; and though without lips, was ever speaking. And Its words were: beauty, harmony and life.

The spirit of the Aton brought with it the greatest art of the Egyptians. For the first time, the sculpturing and painting became alive. No longer men carved only sphinxes with inscrutable eyes, or seated figures majestic but aloof. Akhnaton had found the rhythm and the flow of nature. He saw the Aton moving in the winds and bending the grain in the fields. He saw the palms sway to the breath of the Aton. He beheld in the motion of all things one Life, ever-moving. So, art was for the first time linked to nature. The music in the soul of the dreamer became a music of line, and a deeply satisfying consciousness lifted Egyptian art to the level of great genius. It would be natural that Akhnaton's understanding should affect not only technique but subject matter. The Aton gave dignity to simple things, and Akhnaton was filled with the realization of the beauty and divinity of the commonplace. He elevated therefore the normal circumstances of life to a new standard of significance. He found more of God in the home and the family, and men at their work. He felt it appropriate not to carve great images of heavenly kings with flails, shepherd's crooks, and the scepters of the three worlds. His art was the Aton moving the simple things to rightness. A deeply religious spirit shows through the sculpturing and painting of his period. The Aton is everywhere present, mingling with all things on equal terms, loving the least with the greatest, seated at the poor man's table as surely as at the feast of princes.

The inevitable result of believing in an impersonal, omnipresent, universal Father was a democratic attitude towards all classes of people. The Aton was in the slave, and made even the humblest serf a participant in divinity. If the Aton made no distinction for family or class, neither could he who served the Aton. Thus, democracy came as the natural result of the correct interpretation of the universal plan. If a man correctly understands God and lives that understanding completely, he puts his life and world in order inevitably.

To the Egyptian mind, the problem of death was always deeply significant. In the old religion the souls of those who passed on gathered into a strange universe of gods and demons, to be weighed at last upon the scales of judgment before many-eyed Osiris. Here again, Akhnaton sounded a challenge to all the beliefs of men. He believed the Aton to be everywhere, and those who died departed not from It but remained in It forever. Therefore, there could be no hell, for hate and suffering and doubt had no place in a universe full of love and truth. The Pharaoh believed that those who died lived in a misty world beyond. But in that world also rose the sun of truth, and the souls of the dead turned up their faces to the light, while the countless hands from the rays of the Aton lifted each and sustained each with the ever-living law.

QUOTATIONS FROM THE HYMNS OF AKHNATON

"Oh, living Aton, beginning of life! Though Thou art afar, Thy rays are on earth; though Thou art on high, Thy footprints are the day."

"How manifold are all Thy works, They are hidden from before us, Oh Thou sole god whose powers no other possesseth."

"The birds flutter in the marshes, their wings uplifted in adoration to Thee."

"Thou makest the beauty of form through Thyself alone."

"Thou art in my heart; there is no other that knoweth Thee, save Thy son Akhnaton."

"For Thou art duration, beyond mere limbs; by Thee man liveth."

"The world is in Thy hand, even as Thou hast made them."

"The fish in the river rise to the surface towards Thy face, and Thy rays penetrate the great waters."

"Thou created the earth according to Thy will when Thou wast alone."

"The chick is in its egg cheeping within its shell, Thou givest it breath therein that it may live."

Yours sincerely,

Manly P. Hall

THE FOURTH YEAR OF MANLY P. HALL'S STUDENT LETTERS will begin with the May, 1937 issue. The new series will take up the symbolism of the bible. The first six Letters will be devoted to the Old Testament, and the second six to the New Testament. Those students who are interested in the esoteric doctrines concealed in the Jewish and Christian Scriptures will find this series of Letters of the greatest importance. SEND YOUR SUBSCRIPTION NOW for the new series beginning next May. Price $1.00 for 12 Monthly Lessons.

LOS ANGELES, MAR. 15, 1937

Dear Friend,

ORPHEUS

According to Iamblichus and Proclus, the Grecian theology was derived from the teachings of Orpheus. From Orpheus the doctrine descended to Pythagoras, and from Pythagoras to Plato. These three men together were the founders and disseminators of the Secret Doctrine which had been brought from Asia in the second millennium B.C. In the words of Proclus, "What Orpheus delivered mystically through arcane narrations, this Pythagoras learned when he celebrated orgies in the Thracian Ubethra, being initiated by Aglaophemus in the mystic wisdom which Orpheus derived from his mother Calliope, in the mountain Pangaeus."

Some writers have attempted to maintain that Orpheus was a fabulous person belonging to an early cycle of solar myths. Yet it is incredible that a great system of philosophy, which bound together into a brotherhood of initiates many of the most learned of the classical world, could have been conceived and perfected by an imaginary person. It is far more probable that Orpheus is a deified hero, a priest-magician and philosopher, whose extraordinary exploits won him undying fame.

In time he came to be identified with all mystical learning until at last a mythology sprang up about him, obscuring the historical elements of his life and resulting in a confused tradition of frequently inconsistent accounts. In his introduction to the mystical hymns of Orpheus, Mr. Thomas Taylor, the distinguished classical scholar, enumerates five men who bore the name Orpheus. These, living at widely different times and experiencing a variety of circumstances, came in the end to be confused so that the exploits of one are attributed to the others. The first Orpheus was a Thracian who lived between the twelfth and fourteenth centuries B.C.; the second was an Arcadian; the third was of Odrysius; the fourth, a man of Crotonia; and the fifth was correctly named Camarinaeus, a poet.

If the lives of these various persons were finally combined to form one poetic legend, it becomes easy to understand the conflicting accounts of the birth, life, and death of the hero. The several histories of the death of Orpheus, for example, may well relate to the circumstances surrounding the decease of each of the five poets who bore the sacred name.

It is impossible to discover with certainty the date of the first Orpheus. It is generally agreed, however, that he lived before the fall of Troy and was the original priest-initiate, the most worthy and enlightened of the five. There is considerable dispute as to the exact time of the exodus of the Jews from Egypt. Moses, as the leader of the migration, lived about 1200 B.C. according to one calculation, and about 1400 B.C. according to another. It has been stated that the first Orpheus was a contemporary of Moses. It is certainly true from all accounts that Orpheus lived before the Trojan War. Troy fell B.C. 1184. Edouard Schure in the great initiates writes of Orpheus, "He was contemporary with Moses, five centuries before Homer, and thirteen centuries before Christ."

The homeland of the great bard was Thrace, a wild, heavily forested, and rugged country, sacred to the Gods. In the furthermost recesses of this land were ancient temples to the father divinities of the Greeks. Here aged and bent Cronus had his altars. Here so stood prehistoric stones to Uranus, father of the heavens. Here so were shrines to Pater Zeus and in forest glens, the altars of the nymphs. A strange and weird country was that land where dwelt the hardy Thracians, tending their flocks of sheep and foraging the countryside.

Fabre d'Olivet, a profound scholar in early language and etymology, wrote that the word Thracia was derived from the Phoenician word Rakhiwa, which meant the ethereal space or the firmament. The name of Thrace had a mystic meaning for the poets and initiates of Greece, such as Pindar, Aeschylus, and Plato. It signified to them the land of pure doctrine and of the sacred poetry proceeding therefrom. Philosophically, it pointed to an intellectual region, the sum total of the doctrines and traditions which state that the universe proceeds from a divine intelligence. (See Orpheus by Schure).

From all this, it is apparent that the Greeks intended to convey the idea that Orpheus was born in a divine world, that his home was the heavenly estate, that he partook from birth of the sacred wisdom. In simpler words, he was an initiate, one of that order of seers whose home is heaven, and who wander but a little while as exiles in this mortal sphere.

It is generally written that Orpheus was the son of the god Apollo and Calliope, the Muse of sweet harmonies. Of course, this statement must be taken as allegorical—Apollo as the Holy Spirit and Light is the father of Truth and Wisdom, and the parent of all the good things in the world; Calliope as harmony and music produces the vehicle for incarnation. Thus,

Truth manifested through Music and the Arts is Orpheus, revealed wisdom, perfection made evident through appropriate forms and natures.

Oiagros, King of Thrace, is usually given as the mortal father of the bard. What mortal woman is concealed under the name Calliope will likely never be known. She was probably a Thracian queen, and Orpheus was born of celestial and terrestrial powers. Such an interpretation of the story is consistent with the known practices of the Greek fabulists.

It was openly declared that Pythagoras was the son of Apollo, that he was born of an immaculate conception after being conceived by a Holy Spirit. Pythagoras thus reflects the glory of his Master Orpheus and is accorded a similar divine origin.

The mother of Orpheus was evidently a very talented woman, and like the mother of Confucius, the great sage of China, devoted her life to instructing and perfecting her son in the gentle arts of Music, Poetry, and Song. The fable explicitly states that Orpheus learned music from his mother. His proficiency became so great that his father gave him a lyre with seven strings to play upon. This instrument is the special symbol of the Orphic cult. It represents the universe, nature, and the soul of man. Having received the rudiments of education from his mother, Orpheus is said by some authorities (See Suidas) to have become a disciple of Linus, a man of great knowledge who instructed the youth in the secrets of theology.

Orpheus spent his days in the mountains. The wooded highlands of Thrace echoed with the music of his lyre. Not alone did he charm men with his song, but all nature succumbed to the magic of his spell. The trees stilled the rustle of their leaves, the birds gathered silently on overshadowing boughs while animals came from their lairs, and even the fish in the pools gathered close to the verdant banks listening to the magic of his song. Thus, it came about that Orpheus received the title of The Sweet Singer, and it was reported of him that even the stony heart of the rock was softened by his blessed harmonies.

In distant glens midst the shadows of gnarled oaks, dwelt also the Bacchantes, priestesses of bull horned Dionysus. The Bacchantes were a strange, fierce tribe. Their cries sounded eerily in the somber glens of Mt. Kaoukaion. The soft music of the Orphean lyre gentled the frenzy of the Bacchantes, and their strange company of naiades and satyrs.

ORPHEUS AND EURYDICE

(FROM THE PAINTING BY LORD LEIGHTON)

From their oak groves came these frantic bands. As they approached Orpheus, their cries subsided. Caught in the spell of his divine harmonies, these disciples of ivy-crowned Zagreus fell enraptured at the feet of Orpheus, proclaiming him master singer of the world.

According to Edouard Schure, Orpheus, while still a youth, departed from Thrace to visit Egypt, remaining for twenty years with the priests of Memphis. Here he was initiated, receiving the name Arpha or Orpheus. Schure cites no authority for this account. But it is quite possible that Orpheus did journey into distant lands, and from some highly cultured people obtained the elements of his theology. It is generally admitted by the more profound type of scholars that the Orphic doctrines are of Asiatic origin, with their beginning probably in India.

Wise in all the mysteries of the soul, noble of appearance, and divine of intellect, Orpheus returned to the Thracian soil where he was received with the homage due one of that heroic order between gods and men. The first task of Orpheus the initiate was to reform the rites of Dionysus so that no longer would the priestesses of the order prowl the forest like wild beasts. He restored the sublimity of the ancient religion, brought gravity and integrity to the rites, and among the barbaric Thracians sowed the seeds of a luminous theology which was to change the whole course of civilization.

Orpheus is supposed to have been one of the Argonauts in the quest of the Golden Fleece. The ship Argo, moved by the Orphic lyre, glided gently through the sea, later, the divine music parts the Cyanean rocks, breaks the spell of the sirens, and wakes like sleepers of Lemnos. According to Euripides, Orpheus is the harper who compels the rocks to follow him, and he is referred to as the originator of sacred mysteries. Lucian writes that "Orpheus brought astrology and the magical arts into Greece." From this, it is to be inferred that he studied in distant places and returned to his own land to disseminate the doctrines he had received.

There can be no doubt that a considerable part of the Orphic mysteries is concealed under the allegory of Orpheus and Eurydice. The name Eurydice means "the wide spreading flush of the dawn" thus indicating the myth to be an aspect of the Sun God symbolism. Of all those who listened to the Orphic rhapsodies, Eurydice was most deeply moved. In the legend, Orpheus stirs Eurydice with his song and wins her with his music. Hymenaeus, the god of marriage, was called upon to bless the nuptials of the sweet singer and his bride, but evil omens immediately manifested themselves—the torch smoked, bringing tears to the eyes of the god of marriage.

The fated evil soon materialized. As Eurydice wandered by the shores of dawn, she was seen by a shepherd, by the name Aristaeus. This shepherd, deeply moved by the beauty of Eurydice, made advances to her. She, fleeing from his presence, stepped upon a poisonous snake hidden in the grass. Poisoned in the foot by the bite of night, Eurydice died.

A new song came to the mountains. Orpheus played his grief upon the lyre, and all the hills and valleys wept with him in his bereavement. Even the Gods on high Olympus were moved by the tragedy. But no answer came to the song, and the singer wandered hopeless in the hills, crying out his story to the night.

At last Orpheus determined to seek his lost love in the underworld. He climbed the rocky promontory Taenarus. The gloomy groves echoed his plaintive cry. Orpheus came at last to the mouth of a great cavern which led far down under the mountain into the Stygian realms over which ruled the fearful Hades, god of death. As he descended, he passed bands of spirits wandering aimlessly in the shadow-land. Ghosts, shades of great and noble heroes, and flocks of souls herded by Hermes, psychopomp of the dead, floated by.

At last Orpheus stood before the double throne of the infernal majesty. Pluto and Persephone sat before him, and lifting up his lyre, he sang his plea that Eurydice be given back again to the land of the living. So touching was his song that the ghosts wept, the shades were moved to tears, and all the ghostly company was filled with pity. Tantalus of undying thirst ceased for a moment his struggle for water; Ixion's wheel stopped revolving, and the daughters of Danaus paused in their endless task of drawing water in a sieve. It is said in the mythologies that for the first and only time the cheeks of the Furies were wet with tears.

Great Hades, melted by the song, promised to return Eurydice to the upper-world on one condition, that Orpheus should not look back until they had reached the upper air. The perilous return to the world of the living followed. Up through all the tortuous cavern ways Orpheus led his Eurydice and then, just when it seemed that the journey had been safely ended, he turned back to look at her. A heart-broken cry and Eurydice was swept back again into the vortices of death. In vain, Orpheus sought to return again and plead before the throne of Hades. Eurydice was lost to him forever. He wandered for seven months among the hills, crying his agony to the winds.

As to the life of Orpheus after the death of Eurydice, little is known other than the accounts of his teaching and the establishment of his mysteries. His song was never again without its note of pathos, and his teachings were enriched by the depth of his tragedy.

The legend which has been given herewith is probably founded on a certain measure of truth, based on the description given by Pausanias, that Orpheus, mourning the death of Eurydice, wandered finally to Aornus, a place in Thesprotia, where it was customary to evoke the souls of the dead. Here by magic, he caused his wife to appear but was not able to detain her permanently in the physical world. When she departed again to the abode of night, he died of grief.

The several accounts of the death of Orpheus indicate clearly that they refer to more than one person and may be the faithful accounts of the deaths of the five men who bore the Orphic name. One version describes lightning as the instrument of death. Diogenes, in his verses, writes, "Great Orpheus rests, destroyed by heavenly fire." Schure gives a version to the effect that Orpheus dies of the result of the machinations of Aglaonice, a Thessalian sorceress. The body of the bard was cremated by his disciples and his ashes placed in the temple of Apollo.

It is also reported that he committed suicide, in grief for Eurydice and that nightingales brought forth their young in his tomb, and because of this, of all the birds, have the sweetest voices. Still another version causes him to be destroyed by the Gods for his failure to worship at the shrine of Bacchus, but this story certainly belongs to some later man, for the hymns of Orpheus include nine addressed to Bacchus in his various forms.

The most generally accepted version describes Orpheus wandering heart-broken by the banks of the river Strymon, refusing food and drink. Friends and disciples sought him, trying to bring comfort to his aching heart, but the poet desired only solitude. He, therefore, withdrew to the high mountains Rhodope and Haemus, and there midst the snowy peaks dwelt alone, the lyre his only companion.

Cioconian women in Bacchantic bands roamed these mountains. These, hearing the mournful tone, hastened through the forests and gathered about the musician, inviting him to join in their orgies. Orpheus refused. They continued to beseech him and at last grew angry and threatened him. At last, one of the Bacchantes threw her javelin, but the weapon upon coming within the sound of his song fell harmlessly to the ground. The frenzied women hurled rocks and fired arrows, but no missile would injure the divine musician. The voices of the Bacchantes rose higher and higher and at last their shrill cries drowned out the voice of the singer and the gentle music of his lyre. His protection thus overcome; Orpheus was torn limb from limb by the frantic Bacchantes. They then carried his body and lyre to the river Hebrus, and as the mortal remains of the great poet floated slowly down the stream, the murmur of his lyre could still be heard plaintively singing. The last words of Orpheus were, "Eurydice, Eurydice," and the sever cords of his lyre echoed the sound as they snapped asunder and were silent forever. It is believed that he was in his sixty-third year when he died.

In the tenth book of Plato's republic, there is the vision of Herus Pamphlius. In this it is described that the soul of Orpheus being destined by the law of transmigration to descend into another mortal body chose to be reborn a swan, declaring it chose this creature rather than to be born again of woman because of his tragedy at the hands of the Bacchantes.

THE TEACHINGS OF ORPHEUS

In his introduction to mythical hymns of Orpheus, Thomas Taylor writes, "Orpheus, as Proclus well observes, availing himself of the license of fables, manifests everything prior to Heaven by names, as far as to the first cause. He also denominates the ineffable, who transcends the intelligible unities, Time. And this according to a wonderful analogy, indicating the generation, i.e., the ineffable evolution into light of all things, from the immense principle of all."

According to Orpheus, all existence is suspended from one immeasurable Good—The Sovereign Principle. The cause of all things, denominated The One, is also the Good and the First; the Good because it is the source, the manifestation of the virtues; and the First because it is the summit of all natures, anterior to both the Gods and Nature.

The Orphic concept of God is one of the noblest ever conceived by the human reason—Deity is no longer a person nor an anthropomorphic entity abiding in some empyreal sphere, administering despotic powers over mundane affairs. Gad is revealed as an Eternally Abiding Good, an Ever-Flowing Fountain of Truth and Law, Omnipotent Unity, Omniscient Reality. In this interpretation, Deity is not a being, but a source of beings; not light, but the source of light; not mind, but the source of mind; the hidden origin of all revealed things. Orpheus propitiated That Which Subsists

Upon Itself with hymns of praise and suitable rites. But at no time was The One the object of unthinking devotion or irrational sacrifice.

From the immeasurable effulgency, emerged by procession a splendid triad of supernal qualities.

This triad consists of Being, Life, and Intellect—and is termed The Intelligible Triad. Being is most proximate to The One and is the first manifested virtue of That Which Is Eternal. Life occupies the second place and is prior to intellect. The lowest place is reserved for Intellect, because it is the least indispensable of the qualities.

Being, Life, and Intellect are the first Gods after The One. They abide together in indivisible unity and are properly named the causes of all manifested natures. All forms are rooted in their causes. The universe with its countless genera of evolving lives, is an emergence by progression from super-mundane causes. From the first triad emerge other triads in the following succession:

1. The One.
2. The Intelligible Order.
3. The Intelligible and at the same time Intellectual Order.
4. Intellectual Order.
5. The Super-Mundane Order.
6. The Liberated Order.
7. The Mundane Order.

The first three triads—2, 3, and 4 of the above list—are subjective and causal and self-subsistent. Each of the orders consists of a triad of principles, partaking of the qualities of Being, Life, and Intellect. The third hypostasis of the intellectual triad (number 4 in the list above) is the Demiurgic intellect or the Creator of the mundane world. It is the Demiurgos and his progeny, the original Titans—the fabricative forces, that fashion first the supermundane, then the liberated, and finally the mundane spheres. Therefore, these three spheres are all part of the Demiurgic nature. It is the Demiurgos as the second creator whom the ancients knew as Father, and who was worshipped by the uninformed as the true cause of all things. Most of the theologists and theogonists were unaware of the spiritual orders above the Demiurgos, for which reason they were unable to perceive the true sublimity of the universal plan.

The Mundane Order is the last and lowest of the creative triads. Being, Life and Intellect in this plane are called Zeus, Poseidon, and Hades. These mundane Deities created in turn by virtue of their own establishment the spirit, soul, and form of the material world. Thus, Zeus is called the airy, watery, and earthy father. Zeus, in his aspect of Hades, projects the physical body of Nature. Over this physical body, he rules again in his three, now physical, aspects. In his proper nature as Zeus, he is Lord of the atmosphere, and the sky, and the winds, and the breath. In his second nature as Poseidon, he rules the seas, the streams, and the creatures of the deep. In his third nature as Hades, he rules the earth, the mountains, the caverns, and the deep hidden places, subterranean.

Subterranean Zeus or Hades is merely the creative power manifesting through the physical elements of nature, and the whole physical world becomes, therefore, the body of a wretched dead. This is the meaning of Plato's statement that the body is the sepulcher of the soul and that the soul is prisoned in the body as is the oyster prisoned in its shell. The descent of souls into the sphere of generation or into the realm of infernal Zeus is arcanely set forth in the account of the journey of Orpheus to the underworld in search of Eurydice, who symbolizes experience, soul power, and understanding.

In the Orphic anthropology, man, like the universe, consists of one ineffable principle and six emanating triads of powers or qualities. In this scheme, the mind—or more properly the mental ego which is posited in the lowest division of the intellectual nature—is the Demiurgos or the fabricator of objective forms. Mind, by the Orphic analogy, is, therefore, a little god ruling over lower natures in the same way that the first Gods rule over the whole cosmic plan.

Orpheus taught metempsychosis or the periodic return of soul to the material world. Rebirth was necessary because of the materiality in the soul, which did not die with the dissolution of the body. The passions, appetites, and irrationalities of the soul are not physical, although they are usually dependent upon physical life for their gratification.

The death of the body left the entity with its physical appetites still complete and intense. It was inevitable, therefore, that these appetites should draw the entity back again into physical life. Metempsychosis, therefore, was the law of recurrent involvement in the spheres of sense until the sensory impulses were overcome at their source, the appetitive nature. The physical world exercises a gravitational pull on all natures in which worldliness is dominant. Therefore, the establishment of the Mysteries. These institutions sought to purify the inner life so that man, overcoming his own animal soul, might at death become a blessed spirit "and verge towards the Gods," drawn thereto by the Godliness in his own being.

The sublimity of the Orphic vision is best realized from the contemplation of the rhapsodies devised by the poets of the sacred Mysteries. The Gods are appropriately hymned, their various estates receiving special mention, and their potencies elegantly acclaimed. The verses are like a fine fabric, woven of golden and silken threads, patterned on the looms of the Muses. Orpheus sang the praises of Beauty and Harmony. The Gods could be worshipped with no raucous modes. Man must offer beauty to The Beautiful. He must bring virtues to the altar of the Sovereign Good. The universe is one vast symphony of virtues, and That Which Is The Source Of All Harmony must be harmonically invoked.

The particular symbol of the Orphic cult was the phorminx, the lyre of seven strings, which according to H. P. Blavatsky "is the seven-fold mystery of initiation." It was from the Orphic lyre that Pythagoras derived his inspiration to investigate the music of the spheres. If the seven strings of the phorminx be understood as representing the seven parts of man and the seven divisions of the human soul, then the whole study of harmonics becomes symbolical of inward adjustment. Man, perfecting his own nature, becomes the master musician, drawing divine melodies from the chords of his own being. Chording is combining—it is bringing harmonic values together according to law and rule, living is likewise a science of combining factors into pleasant or unpleasant patterns. The master musician is the one who can play most perfectly the sacred compositions upon the musical instrument of his own perfected life.

After the death of Orpheus, his lyre was suspended in the Temple of Apollo, where it remained a great time universally admired. At last, there came to the temple Neanthus, the son of Pittacus, who, learning of the magical powers of the Orphic lyre, sought to gain possession of it. He bribed one of the priests to substitute a replica for the original instrument and departed from the city, concealing the enchanted lyre under his robes. Arriving at a safe distance, he stopped in a forest, attempting to play the sacred melodies. His untutored fingers produced only discords, however, and he was torn to pieces by wild dogs, who gathered, enraged at his inharmonic sounds. By this, the Greek fabulists implied that when the mystical theology comes into the hands of the profane and is perverted, the evil destroys itself and him who perpetrates it.

It is also recorded that the head of Orpheus gave oracles after the body had been destroyed. The eyes opened, and the lips spoke words inspired. The philosophers explained this legend by saying that Orpheus represents the great doctrine or body of tradition. The temples of this doctrine, the body of Orpheus, were destroyed by the frenzy of the untutored mobs, who always perverted mystic things. The head of Orpheus is the source of this tradition, and although the priestcrafts were dispersed and the altar fires grew cold, still the sacred Truths remained to inspire other generations. Wisdom, the head of Orpheus, never dies, though the body of that wisdom be lost. Therefore, it is said that the head continued to speak after the form had been torn asunder by the frantic Bacchantes.

Orpheus is commonly regarded as the founder, or at least the principal reformer, of the Bacchic and Dionysian Mysteries. It is said of him that he brought the Dionysian Rites from the East, promulgating them among the peoples of Thrace, from which they spread to Attica, and finally permeated most of the Grecian states.

Prior to the Orphic dispensation, the Greeks possessed only an immature concept of the state of the soul after death. To the prehistoric Hellenes, the dead wandered endlessly in a subterranean shadow-land; the hero and the slave came to a common end. Neither virtue of action nor profundity of thinking could rescue the soul from its hopeless roaming in the abode of shadows. An endless parade of shades flowed through the portals of the underworld. At the gate, stood three-headed Cerberus, who snarled viciously at the ghosts floating by. Primitive men believed the tomb of the burial mound to be the gate of a subterranean world and all finally came to that gloomy portal, of which the Chaldeans write, "The hinges are rusty, and the lintels are heavy with dust." This was the underworld of Homer. Heroes all came at the end of silence. Not even great Achilles, brave Nestor, or brave Agamemnon could hope for a better future.

The significance of the Orphic reform thus becomes apparent. It changed man's whole concept of his own destiny. It banished forever the world of shades and its fearful ruler and revealed a divine, benevolent plan, circumscribing all of the vicissitudes of life. Men, learning more about their Gods, discovered more to venerate and to admire. Life was no longer hopeless; great purposes came to be dimly visible. Philosophers dreamed about these purposes, poets sang them, orators discoursed of them—until, at last, the Orphic urge produced the most perfect thinker of classical antiquity, the immortal Plato, in whose realization all the wonders of the universe were understood.

A FEW SELECTED LINES FROM THE ORPHIC RHAPSODIES

These verses are attributed to both Orpheus and the early initiates of his school. It is impossible at this late time to determine the true author of these hymns.

To Musaeus:

Learn, O Musaeus, from my sacred song
What rites most fit to sacrifice belong.
Jove I invoke, the earth, and solar light,
The moons pure splendour, and the stars of night.

* * * *

Illustrious Providence, the noble train
Of daemon forms, who fill th' etherial plain;
Or live in air, in water, earth, or fire,
Or deep beneath the solid ground retire.
To Night (The Fumigation With Torches.)
Night, the great tamer both of Gods and men,
To whom I fled, preserv'd me from his wrath;
For he swift Night was fearful to offend.
Hear, blessed Venus, deck'd with starry light,
In Sleep's deep silence dwelling Ebon night!
To Heaven (The Fumigation From Frankincense.)
Great Heav'n, whose mighty frame no respite knows,
Father of all, from whom the world arose;
Hear, bounteous parent, source and end of all,
Forever whirling round this earthly ball;
Abode of Gods, whose guardian pow'r surrounds
Th' eternal world with ever during bounds;

Whose ample bosom, and encircling folds
The dire necessity of nature holds. To Law (A Hymn.)
The holy king of Gods and men I call,
Celestial Law, the righteous seal of all:
The seal which stamps whate'er the earth contains,
And all conceal'd within the liquid plains:
Stable, and starry, of harmonious frame,
Preserving laws eternally the same.
To The Divinity of Dreams (The Fumigation From Aromatics.)
Thee I invoke, blest pow'r of dreams divine,
Angel of future fates, swift wings are thine.
Great source of oracles to human kind,
When stealing soft, and whisp'ring to the mind,
Thro' sleep's sweet silence, and the gloom of night,
Thy pow'r awakes th' intellectual sight.

Yours sincerely,

Manly P. Hall

LOS ANGELES, APRIL, 1937

Dear Friend,

HERMES TRISMEGISTUS

Dear Friend: The burning of the Alexandrian Libraries resulted in the destruction of most of the historical records of the Ancient World. From all parts of the earth the most valuable of books, scrolls, and tablets had been diligently gathered and housed in several great buildings, especially the Bruckion and Serapeum. When Cleopatra stood in the presence of the mountain of burned manuscripts, she wept for the lost glory of the world.

The modern Egyptologist possesses but limited facilities to assist him in his effort to restore the sublime theology of the ancient Egyptians. For the most part, the surviving literature of these people consists of mortuary rolls, most of these merely variants of the book of the Dead according to the various recensions. The Egyptian priestcraft guarded its secrets carefully, and so thoroughly were the Mysteries protected that only an occasional fragment has survived to the present day.

Among the principal deities of the Egyptian pantheon is Thoth, or Tahuti, or Theuth. In the Osiris Cycle Thoth. is the friend of Nut, the mother of Osiris. When Nut is cursed by Ra and forbidden to deliver her children on any of the days of the year, Thoth plays a game of dice with the moon Goddess Selene and wins from her a seventieth part of her light. With this part he made five days, which did not belong to the calendar and are called inter-calendry and which he added to the previous Egyptian year that consisted of 360 days. On these five days the children of Nut were born, and because of this these days were always regarded as sacred by the Egyptians who would transact no business on them but reserved them for festivals. Thus, in the early mythology of the Egyptians, Thoth assumes his true role of teacher, protector, and God of Learning. He is the deity who devises means by which all divine concerns can be accomplished. It is Thoth who aids Isis in the administration of the kingdom while Osiris travels in distant countries. After the murder of Osiris, it is Thoth who, assists Isis in the performance of her queenly duties and becomes, in turn, the mentor of Horus the Child. As Chiron was the preceptor of Achilles, so Thoth was the teacher of Horus and fitted him for the great battle against Typhon, the usurper of the empire.

It is customary to regard Hermes as the Grecianized form of Thoth and to assume that Thoth in his attributes as Hermes returned to Egypt under the Ptolemies to win new veneration as founder of the Hermetic sciences. A careful consideration of the Grecian Hermes forces one to the realization, however, that it is most unlikely that the two deities are identical. It is true that Hermes was the Messenger of the Gods, according to the Hellenes; and that his worship was carried to Rome where he was named Mercury and usually represented with winged cap and sandals.

The Latin Mercury was merely an intermediary between the Gods and man. The Egyptian Thoth has an entirely different estate. He is the personification of Wisdom; he is the very intellect of the Great God who formed the world. He is not a messenger but a teacher. It is true that he is a bearer of divine secrets, but he participates fully therein and is in his own right both an Initiator and the First Initiate, revealing knowledge from his own inexhaustible supply, As Lord of the Writing Tablet, as bearer of the Stylus, he is frequently depicted as Ibis-headed recording the judgments of the dead before the throne of Osiris.

Yet Thoth as the God of Wisdom, Hermes as the Messenger of the Gods, and Winged Mercury, all fall short of being the Hermes of the Hermetists, the immortal mortal who, according to one writer, was the author of 30,000 books.

Most authorities on the subject of Egyptian metaphysics have taken it for granted that the Egyptian Hermes was an entirely mythological person, a god accumulated out of the tradition of centuries and finally accepted as the personification of all knowledge; especially of the sciences and arts. It is doubtful, however; whether this conclusion is entirely consistent with facts. It appears far more likely that this Hermes was a deified mortal who lived at some remote time and conferred unusual cultural benefits upon the people of Egypt.

For our present purpose, therefore, let us accept the Alexandrian Hermes as an entity separate from the mythological Thoth or the divine messenger of the Greek and Latin legends. That he may not be confused with these others, let us name him by the titles most frequently accorded him in the first centuries of the Christian era. These were Hermes Trismegistus or Mercurius Ter Maximus. This Hermes, The Thrice Greatest, was identified as a person by Plato, who refers to him as an Egyptian Theuth and implies that he was a great learned man who lived in the antiquity of the Egyptian people. This man is by some writers believed to have been a king of the Egyptians, belonging to the divine dynasty which preceded human rulership's. He is also spoken of as a high priest of the Egyptian temple, whose pontificate extended through the reign of Pharaoh Ammon. This last implication suggests that the other gods worshipped by the Egyptians as spiritual beings may have been deified heroes who ruled over the people in prehistoric times.

It is exceedingly difficult to assign any reasonable date for Hermes. Cicero gives us a clue to the situation when he declares that the fifth Mercury slew Argus and fled for protection to Egypt. Arriving in this distant country, he gave up his life to educating its people. Among the arts and sciences which he established were writing, history, mathematics, art, medicine, law, religions, astronomy, chemistry, astrology, divination, architecture, and chronology. He set down the rules for kings, determined the rights of peoples, taught how land and properties should be divided, worked out the system of measurements and weights, and founded the city of Hermopolis. This would be an extensive group of labors for a mythical person to accomplish. In fact, it may be reasonable to assume that this was far more than even a highly enlightened human being could have done.

When Cicero speaks of five Mercuries, the answer becomes apparent—severed persons, probably living over a period of centuries or even thousands of years and accorded similar title, have been merged into the one, and this one has descended in the memory of man as the most profound, ingenious, and diversified of intellects, the personification of all knowledge and all thought.

Most ancient historians were of the opinion that the historical Hermes, whom Cicero calls the fifth Mercury, was a contemporary of Moses. Some give him an even greater antiquity and acknowledge him to have lived in the second millennium B.C.. Efforts have been made to prove that he was Moses, but there is nothing tangible to sustain such an opinion. Nor is there any proof that the older Hermetic writings were particularly indebted to the Jewish metaphysical systems. Hermeticism is evidently indigenous to the Egyptians. The Gods of Egypt are given first place in the Hermetic theology, and the older doctrine attributed to Hermes is built up around the Osiris Cycle and the great Gods of Hermopolis.

The Initiate Priest of the Egyptians,
HERMES TRISMEGISTUS

There is not the slightest surviving hint as to the parentage of Hermes or the circumstances surrounding his birth or early life. If the Greeks legends of Mercury are of any importance, it may be inferred that he was of royal or, at least, noble ancestry and enjoyed all the advantages of his day. In the Arab traditions, Hermes is the disciple of the mysterious being called Agathodaemon. This name is usually associated with supernatural being, but it is possible that Hermes was the disciple of some very wise sage or hierophant of ancient Egyptian Mysteries.

The oldest likenesses of Hermes, and these are of no great antiquity, depict him as a tall man, dressed in flowing robes of Greek rather than Egyptian style. He is usually represented wearing a turban wrapped around a conical MITRE-like helmet. He is bearded and of venerable appearance, and is usually surrounded by the symbols of his cult. The picture which illustrates this article was drawn by the celebrated engraver of mystical and theosophical works, Theodore de Bry. The plate was cut in the early years of the seventeenth century and is one of the best examples of the appearance attributed to Hermes.

Kenealy in Enoch, the second messenger of god tries to prove that Hermes was the Enoch of the Jews. But the opinions of Kenealy, like those of an earlier mythologist, Bryant, who believed Hermes to be Cadmus of the Greeks, are entirely speculative and are not supported by tangible evidence. From Hermetic writings, it appears that the ministry of Hermes was preceded by a vision or an illumination. This illumination is recorded in the divine pymander, or as it is more commonly called, the shepherd of men. After the vision, Hermes went forth to convert the world to the great truths. Thus preached The Thrice Greatest:

"O people of the earth, men born and made of the elements, but with the spirit of the Divine Man within you, rise from your sleep of ignorance! Be sober and thoughtful. Realize that your home is not on the earth but in the Light. Why have you delivered yourselves over unto death, having the power to partake of immortality? Repent, and change your minds. Depart from the dark light and forsake corruption forever. Prepare yourselves to climb through the Seven Rings to-blend your souls with the eternal Light."

The sermon of Hermes seems to have been spoken directly to certain disciples, but there is evidence that he went up and down the land, staff in hand, teaching, guiding, and calling men to the life of wisdom.

In one discourse, Hermes addresses his son Tatian, but whether this is to be taken literally cannot be ascertained. Tatian may have been only a disciple to whom Hermes spoke as a father in wisdom. The inferences in the texts regarding this matter are not clear, and it is quite possible that Tatian was actually a son. From the divine pymander, we gain the impression that Hermes lived a long and useful life and died of natural causes, for it is said that "at last came the evening of his life." On this occasion, he gathered disciples about him and preached a last discourse. The great adept concluded his sermon with:

"Blessed art Thou, O Father! The man Thou hast fashioned would be sanctified with Thee as Thou hast given him power to sanctify others with Thy Word and Thy Truth."

There is only one other fragment of information available. Albertus Magnus, the great Catholic Father, wrote that Hermes was buried in the valley of Ebron and that Alexander the Great visited the tomb which was in a cave. At the order of Alexander, the grave was opened. It was found that the body of the master had turned to dust. Where the body had lain rested a great emerald that had been buried with the magus. The emerald contained the secrets of the Hermetic art deeply embossed upon its surface. It is called Tabula Smaragdina Hermetis and it is believed the stone was artificially made, having been cast in a mold and fixed by alchemical processes to the hardness and color of a genuine emerald.

The writing upon the gem includes a statement of analogy, which is the principal key to the Hermetic sciences. Simply translated, it reads:

"That which is above is like unto that which is below, and that which is below is like unto that which is above."

In the literature of the Egyptians, there is a curious story of the lost books of Hermes, which had been deposited in the bed of the Nile within nested caskets. The books were guarded by strange monsters and contained upon their hieroglyphically adorned pages all the secrets of magic, such as the invocations of spirits, prayers for the dead, and incantations to be used on all occasions to bring about secretly desired purposes.

It is worth noting that Hermes was one of the few pagan philosophers who was not attacked by the early Christian Church. He is accepted as a true messenger of God, a great prophet, and his books were in considerable demand among the priests of the North African Church. In his stromata, Clement of Alexandria describes the forty-two books of Hermes which were carried by the priests in religious processions. He says that one book of Hermes contained hymns to the Gods, the second, the regulations for the life of a king. Then there were four relating to fixed stars, the sun and the moon, the conjunctions and risings of the heavenly bodies. He mentions also ten books of honors to the Gods and ten called hieratic, which embodied the laws, and six treating of disease. It is extraordinary that these works which existed in the first centuries of the Christian era should have entirely disappeared so that no copy in the Egyptian language is known to exist. There can be but one answer: the books were jealously guarded by the priests, were destroyed or hidden at the time the religion declined so that they would escape profanation at the hands of the unworthy.

The Hermetic books now known are probably only late versions of older writings. The divine pymander, which is the most important of the Hermetic fragments, does not seem to have been known earlier than the second century, A.D. This has led to the belief that the Hermetic books were actually written after the beginning of the Christian era by a scholar or a group of scholars, profoundly versed in ancient lore and tradition. It seems to me, however, that there is a deep inspirational quality about these writings which suggests a high and sacred origin. They are too noble intrinsically to be the production of ordinary mortals. It seems more likely that the older works were fading from the memory of man, and an effort was made to preserve this memory and save the old wisdom from disappearing entirely under the pressure of early Christian proselyting.

Nor is it fair to say that the doctrines of Hermes are plagiarized from the Christian revelation. A deep examination shows that whoever wrote or compiled the Hermetic dialogues was not a Christian nor was he greatly influenced by Christian opinion. The whole production is distinctly pagan, but deeply and reverently so. The pymander can stand beside any sacred book of the world and is equal to any in the sheer beauty of its composition and the luminousness of the doctrines which it expounds. There can be no doubt that the Hermetic philosophy was the product of a noble, transcendent soul who, indeed, walked with God in some distant age. In the words of Longfellow:

"Trismegistus! three times greatest!

How thy name sublime!

Has descended to this latest Progeny of time!"

The principal source of the Hermetic doctrines is the pymander, or vision. This sets forth a complete system of metaphysical theology and philosophy. Certain other dialogues and fragments with the pymander make up the corpus hermeticum. Nearly all of the Hermetic books are under controversy. Scholars differ widely as to the period of their composition and their place in the religious literature of the world. It is generally acknowledged by most experts that the Hermetic writings in their present form are of no great antiquity. They were apparently unknown to the Egyptians prior to the Christian era and first came into prominence in the third and fourth centuries A.D., although they were probably in circulation as early as the first century A.D.

If these various opinions are in substance correct, and they are the result of extensive scholarship, there must remain a grave doubt as to the authenticity of even the pymander. It is almost certain that the entire Hermetic literature that has survived to this day is but a restatement of much older tradition now hopelessly lost. It is extraordinary in itself that the name Hermes should be known throughout the world and yet neither the records of his life nor even his words have survived. Hermes has become a patron of learning associated with all wisdom, and it is in this capacity that his name has lived.

It is also significant that the Hermetic doctrines, though frequently referred to, have never assumed definite shape but remained themselves a sort of shadowy force entirely abstract and obscure. In the earlier times, Hermeticism seems to have been cosmologic and regenerative. Later it took on the appearance of alchemy and chemistry. Even the Qabalah and the Pythagorean mathematical teachings were included in its province, and at last in this generation the word has become synonymous with all Metaphysics, New Thought, Transcendentalism, and even Spiritualism. This wide diffusion is due to man's lack of actual knowledge of the original teachings of Hermes. Where nothing is known everything is suspected; and a dignified name has been frequently attached to unmeritorious undertakings.

For our present purpose, I think we should limit our consideration of Hermeticism to certain well-defined phases of the subject. We shall, therefore, consider two headings: the older Hermetic which we shall designate the philosophical, and the later Hermetic which we shall call alchemical. The earlier school is the most authentic, and the writings of the second group are distinctly apocryphal. The principal doctrines of the philosophical are as follows:

Hermes taught that the universe was sustained through the energies of certain secondary Gods who were the manifestors and administrators of the Divine Will. Of the First God, the recondite Source of all things, Hermes says little, regarding this matter as too profound to be discovered by intellectual process. Although Hermes did not define the First Cause, he seems to prefer to denominate it the Primordial Mind, or the Supreme Being from whom emanated Reason, the sustainer and orderer of all natural phenomena. Thus, Hermes was monotheistic in principle and pantheistic in his concept of the secondary principles, which emerging from the one become the sustaining power administering to the many.

In this concept Hermes parallels Plato who in slightly different words expresses the same thought, thus revealing the secret of mythologies. The ancient pantheons of divinities are really the personifications of the various attributes of Universal Life. The Universal One first emanates superior beings and with these, Its first progeny, rules over the mundane sphere and its creatures. This mundane sphere and all that it bears upon itself belongs to secondary emanations and is, therefore, less proximate to the Divine Reason.

The Gods, or administrators who do the will of the Father, circulate through their own natures the heavenly fire which is the life of all things. These first Gods are, therefore, the planets and stars who move in orbits or within certain boundaries. These orbits are called thrones and from their fiery rings the Governors rule the sublunary sphere, controlling it by the strange force which Hermes calls destiny. Thus, in the Hermetic teachings, we have an authority for the ancient belief in astrology. The planetary Governors, ruling terrestrial concerns, manifest by Their ponderous motions and mutual combinations the purposes or the will of the Great Mind.

In cosmogony, the Hermetic system is probably either the source or the principal determining factor in the Ptolemaic theory. The earth is placed in the center, the planets and the luminaries circle around the earth in orbits which the Egyptians symbolized by the cross-section of the onion. Beyond the orbits of the planets was the circle of the fixed stars which constituted the wall of heaven or the outer boundary of the mundane complex. This is the system which is used in the Revelation of St. John and forms the working key to nearly all occult cosmogonies. St. John going through the little door in the wall of heaven emerges into the empyrean or the divine world outside the bubble of the cosmos.

According to Hermes, the orbits of the seven planets (known to the ancients) formed a ladder connecting heaven with earth, and conversely, earth with heaven. This was the sacred Ladder of Seven Rungs, the Ladder of Jacob, and also the Ladder of Golden Cords by which Mohammed ascended to the footstool of God in the celebrated Night Journey. The planets are also the Seven Seals of Revelation which must be opened, the Seven Gates of the Mithraic Mysteries. They are the Seven Trumpets and the Seven Vials, and the Seven Churches which are in Asia. The powers which emanate from them are the Seven Cardinal Virtues, and the perversions of these powers are the Seven Deadly Sins. They are the Seven Sacraments, the Seven Elohim of the Jews, the Seven Great Gods of the Egyptians, the Cabiri of Samothrace, Ildabaoth and his six Sons, the Titans, the Seven Logoi, in fact, all the mysterious septenary powers of antiquity. In the pymander it is described that upon their thrones sat the Seven Governors administering the whirlwind of the cosmic power.

When the divine emanations were complete, the One Mind caused nature and the lower elements to be manifested out of Its own Being, and It established nature on its eternal foundations, gave it to the Governors to be ruled over with eternal wisdom. And nature out of its yearnings brought forth life, creeping and crawling things, and creatures of the deep, and soulless monsters who had forms but were too distant from the Light to have souls. Out of the strivings of the earth, came forth also dragons and monsters and the strange creatures described by Berosus. Thus, was nature formed, and the Governors gave it shape, but it did not live because the Great Mind had not bestowed life.

And in Its wisdom, the Supreme Mind, Father of all things, fashioned Mari, a superior and beautiful creature made in the likeness of the Light and full of effulgency in all its parts. And this Man dwelt with the Father, and like unto the Father, to this Man was given dominion not only over the world but over the Governors of the world. (This reminds us of the story of the infant Bacchus to whom Zeus gave the universe as a plaything, or Dionysus who was presented with the spinning top which he might whirl forever.) And the Governors bowed down to the Man who had been fashioned, the metaphysical Man who had no body but was all soul. And each of the Governors bestowed upon the Man one of His qualities so that He gained inwardly seven natures, which were gifts of the Gods of the Seven Worlds.

Now, this divine Man, gazing down into the deep, saw the physical world as though it were a mirror or a smooth ocean, and He beheld his own likeness shadowed in the deep, and like Narcissus in the Greek legend, He became enamored of his own shadow and desired to descend unto it. Thus, desire came into being, and with desire came the fulfillment of it, for that which Mind desires It accomplishes. And the Man descended into the abyss, He entered into the shadow, and the shadow entered into Him, and the Mind which had been above the Mystery became part of the Mystery, and the lower world received the Mind, and the creatures of the abyss became mind-full and the Man forgot His kinship with the Light and began to struggle outwardly to gain that which was its own inner nature.

Ages passed, the One Man had become humanity, and all human beings together were one supermundane entity, and in all men was the longing of the One—to be returned to the Light. The seven principles which the Seven Governors had bestowed upon the Divine Man had become seven bodies or physical principles, and the Governors, wording upon their own principles in man, enslaved him, and left him victim of the limitations which bodies and senses impose.

Such was the state of affairs when Hermes, sitting alone on the side of a mountain, received the vision. The heavens parted, and the Dragon of Wisdom stood before him, and the Dragon Poimandres said:

"I Thy God am the Light and the Mind which were before substance was divided from Spirit and darkness from Light."

Hermes bowed to the Great One and besought Poimandres to reveal the way by which men might be restored again to the Light, and Poimandres replied:

"The path of immortality is hard, and only a few find it. The rest await the Great Day when the wheels of the universe shall be stopped and the immortal spares shall escape from the sheaths of substance. Woe unto those who wait, for they must return again, unconscious and unknowing, to the seed-ground of stars, and await a new beginning. Those who are saved by the light of the mystery which I have revealed unto you, O Hermes, and which I now bid you to establish among men, shall return again to the Father who dwelleth in the White Light, and shall deliver themselves up to the Light and shall be absorbed into the Light, and in the Light they shall become Powers in God. This is the Way of Good and is revealed only to them that have wisdom."

In the vision it is further described how the Truth-seeker, climbing the ladder of the stars returns to the Governors that portion of their natures which was derived from them. Thus, he returns to the Sun and its Lord his ambitions, to Mars and its Governors his boldness, to Jupiter his wealth—until at last purified of all temporal things, the soul escapes from the rings because there is nothing left of the nature of the rings in itself. Until such time as this escape is possible, life and death are merely alternatives between an embodied and disembodied state. But whether physically alive or physically dead, the entity remains in the natural world. Only wisdom can release it from the rings of temporality to the empyreal diffusion where dwells the Supreme Mind. Therefore, we may say that the Hermetic philosophy in its older form is a redemptive teaching, leading man to a state of well-being through the practice of virtues and through rites of purification.

The later Hermetic school was founded upon the doctrines of Hermes which circulated among the eclectics of Alexandria and later among the Arabs and, drifting back into Europe through the Dark Ages, assumed an almost exclusively chemical terminology and interpretation. The difference between the philosophical and alchemical schools may be more apparent than real, but certainly for the alchemists of the Middle Ages Hermes was a transputer of metals and not a redeemer of men.

Thousands of sincere human souls, built furnaces in their spare rooms and became a prey to a violent and insidious superstition. The street of the goldmakers at Prague is an example of a road faced on either side by the houses of alchemists. Man, ever elevating the temporal state above his divine expectations, brewed and distilled, evaporated and condensed, fermented and decomposed practically every substance distinguishable to the senses in the hope that by some amazing dispensation he would find a lump of purest gold in his furnace. Hundreds of writers called upon the Hermetic Gods for aid, and numerous chemical formulas accredited to Hermes himself were published and distributed to an avid populace.

It probably all began when some chemist-philosopher discovered the secrets of human regeneration could appropriately be concealed under a chemical terminology. Gold was Spirit or God; the seven base metals were the powers of the seven Governors; the retort was the human body; the fire was aspiration; and the tortured chemicals seething in the bottles aptly illustrated man's troublous state. But the moment you clothe any idea in a symbolism, a certain part of mankind will lack the penetration to discover the real under the figure. As a result, Hermetic science descended into a frenzied effort to find the powder of projection, the elixir of life, and the philosopher's stone.

One alchemist announced that one grain of this powder would transmute into purest gold one hundred thousand times its own weight. But his readers did not realize that this powder is wisdom, one grain of which can transmute all the ignorance in the world. Nor did the reader properly understand that the philosopher's stone is knowledge, the great miracle worker, or that the elixir of life was Truth, which makes all things new. It was sad that misunderstandings should exist, but wherever great truths are given to small minds, misunderstandings are inevitable. Thus, in mediaeval literature, the word Hermetic means actually chemical, or, more correctly, philosophy in terms of chemistry.

Of the later Hermetic philosophers, the most important were probably the Rosicrucian's and the Paracelsists. The Rosicrucian Order was composed of persons who had come to realize that the Hermetic arcanum was a cleverly concealed story of human regeneration. Deeply thoughtful men, not to be intrigued by the promise of material gold, discovered and set forth the secret keys to the chemical fable. Having restored the philosophy they sought to privately circulate it among the learned of Europe in the hope that it would bring about in the end the transmutation of empires and would tincture with the fire of immortality the crumbling creeds and cults that lived on from age to age unaware of their divine birthright.

There is a divine science hidden under the chemical writings of such men as Paracelsus, van Helmont, Ripley, Roger Bacon, and Nicholas Flamel. There can be no doubt that these men were genuine Hermetic adepts who, realizing that pearls must not be cast before swine, wrote obscurely but included in their writing's sufficient hints and suggestions that the worthy would not be deceived. Each man read into the writing that which was his own vision. Some, therefore, sought the redemption of themselves, but most lived on striving with athanor and alembic for the fabled red lion and the hope of terrestrial immortality.

QUOTATIONS

"Listen within yourself and look into the infinitude of Space and Time. There can be heard the songs of the Constellations, the voices of the Numbers, and the harmonies of the Spheres."

"To know divine thought, O souls, you descend and painfully ascend the path of the seven planets and of their seven heavens."

"The sleep of the body is the sober watchfulness of the mind and the shutting of my eyes reveals the true Light."

"Holy is God, who is determined that He shall be known and who is known by His own to whom He reveals Himself."

"My silence is filled with budding life and hope, and is full of good. My words are the blossoms of fruit of the tree of my soul. For this is the faithful account of what I receive from my true Mind, through whom I became inspired by God with the Truth. Since that day my Mind hath been ever with me and in my own soul it hath given birth to the Word: The Word is Reason, and Reason hath redeemed me."

Yours sincerely,

Manly P. Hall

AUTHOR AND MANAGING EDITOR

Darrell Jordan is an acolyte of the August Fraternity, former Noble Grand-IOOF and Freemason. He is also a member of the Theosophical and Philalethes Societies.

Darrell Jordan

BOOKS BY THE AUTHOR

- Illustrations of Masonry
- Surviving Document of the Widow's Son
- The Undiscovered Teachings of Jesus
- The Initiates
- Jefferson's Bible
- Master Masons Handbook
- Forgotten Essays - W.L. Wilmshurst
- Forgotten Essays - Waite
- Forgotten Essays - H. Stanley Redgrove
- The Writings of Sigismond Bacstrom M.D.
- Forgotten Essays – Reincarnation
- Masonic Writings of George Oliver
- Masonic Lectures by Wellins Calcott
- The Fellowcraft Handbook
- Secret Societies
- Vibration and Life
- Key to the Rosicrucian Characters
- The Revelation of John
- Life and the Ideal
- The Philosophical History of Freemasonry
- The Magic of the Middle Ages
- Musings of a Chinese Mystic
- The Life of the Soul
- Christian Mysticism
- Krishna and Orpheus
- The Eleusinian Mysteries & Rites
- The Crucifixion Letter
- The Mystic Key
- You Paid What?
- The Illustrated Pioneer History of the America
- Montana Freemasons 19th Century
- Washington Freemasons 19th Century
- Idaho Freemasons 19th Century
- Rock Metaphysics
- Emblems: Jean Jacque Boissard and Otto van Veen
- Emblems: Nicholas M. Meerfeldt
- Alchemy Art: Manly P. Hall
- Emblems: Manly P. Hall
- Alchemy Art & Symbols
- Splendor Solis

For the latest information, please visit author's book site:

Parallel47North.com/collections/esoteric-books

If you have any question, suggestion, or feedback, please contact:

info@Parallel47North.com

MANLY P. HALL BOOK SERIES

All Seeing Eye Book Series

A Seeker of More Intelligent Life Book Series

Hand-drawn Illustration of Manly P. Hall and Book Cover Art by Jessica Naomi.

The Artist Portfolio: JessicaNaomiDesigns.com

www.ingramcontent.com/pod-product-compliance
Lightning Source LLC
Chambersburg PA
CBHW020310010526
44107CB00001B/49